The family of Shel Silverstein is proud to celebrate the twenty-fifth anniversary of *Different Dances*. Long out of print, this new edition is for readers who may recall its impact when first published in 1979 and for those unfamiliar with Shel's adult work. We lovingly remember Shel's unique artistry, insight, and wisdom with this provocative collection from the '50s, '60s, and '70s, which remains timeless and true.

August 2004

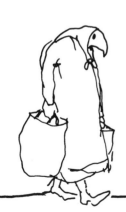

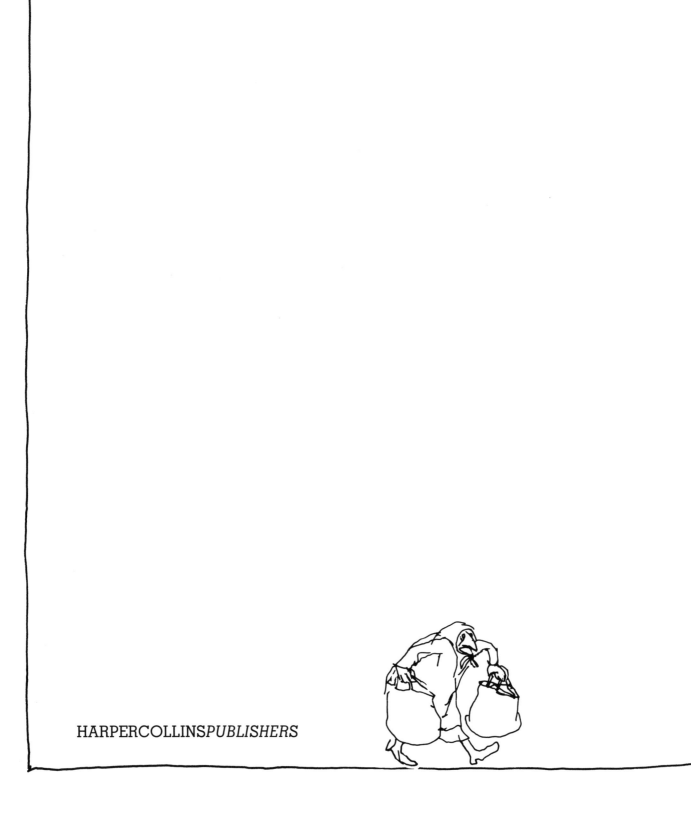

HARPERCOLLINS*PUBLISHERS*

Silverstein

Different Dances

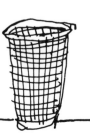

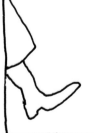

For information address HarperCollins Publishers, 195 Broadway, New York, NY 10007.
www.harpercollinschildrens.com

Library of Congress Catalog Card Number: 78-19473   ISBN 978-0-06-055430-9

25TH ANNIVERSARY EDITION, 2004
16 17 SCP 10 9 8 7 6

For Herb

THE BAG LADY

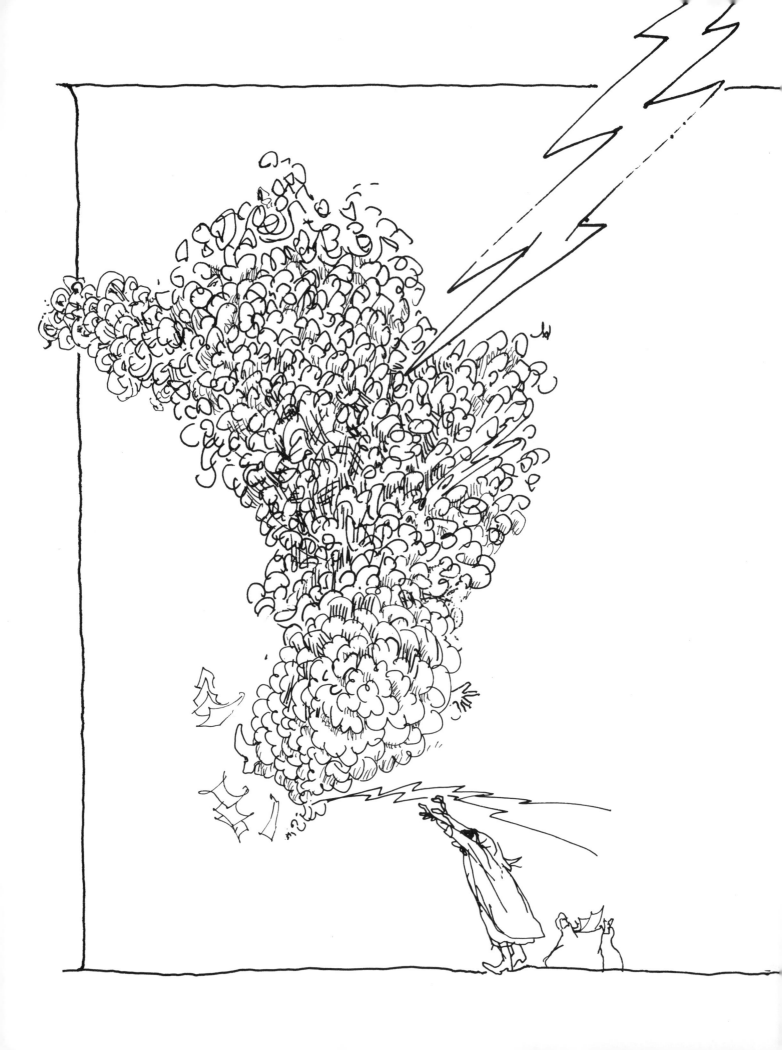

THE MEAT GRINDER

KEEPING TIME

THE ARTIST

DISTORTION

THE ACTOR

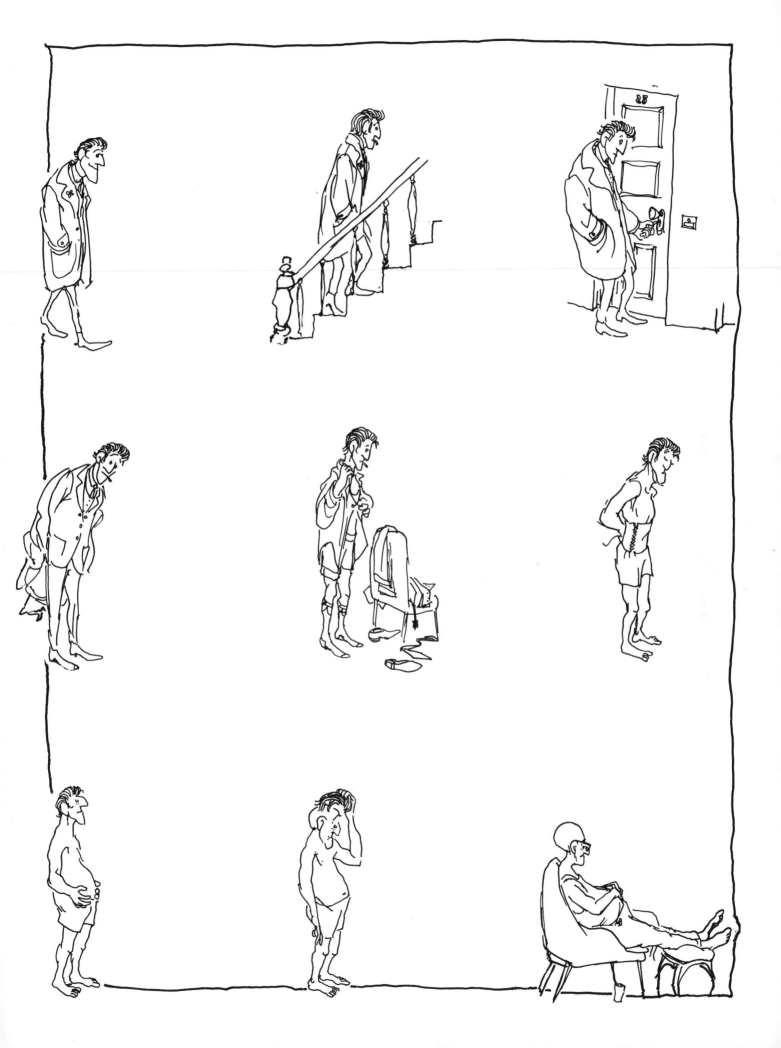

COME LIVE WITH ME

THE QUIET MAN

DAUGHTER, BEWARE
OF MEN BEARING PEDESTALS

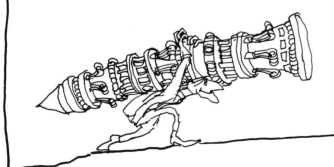

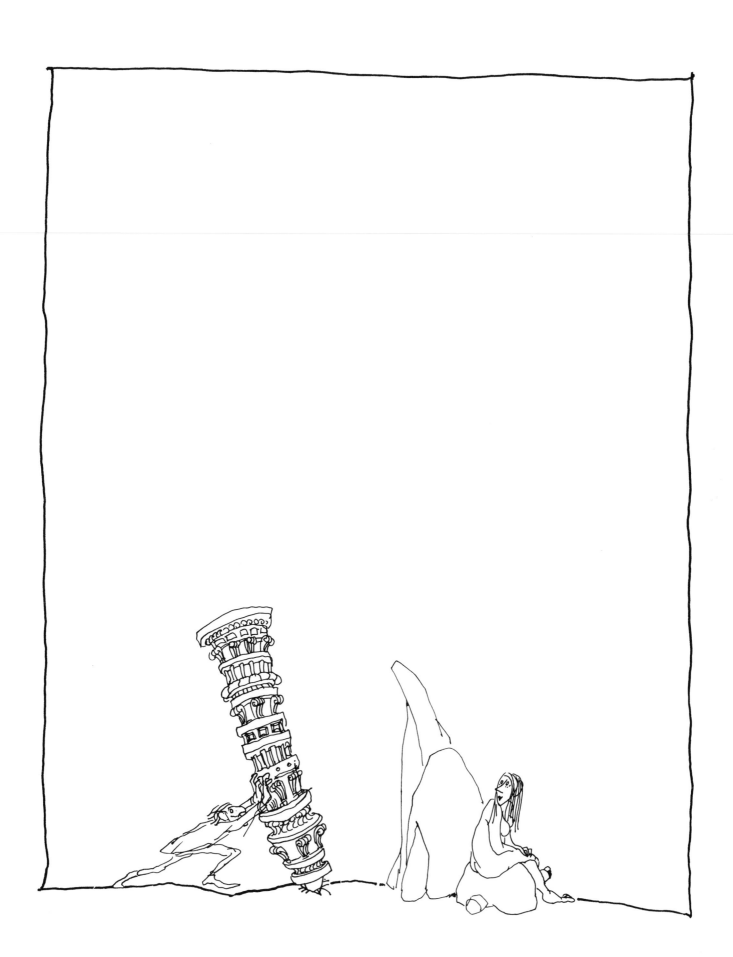

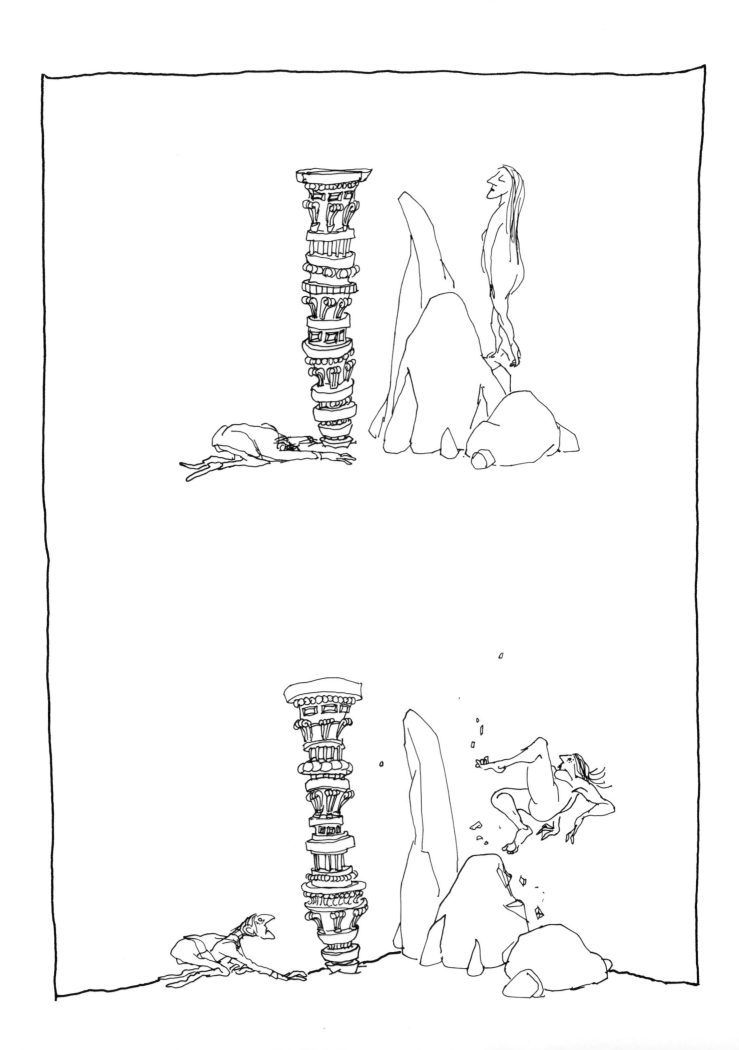

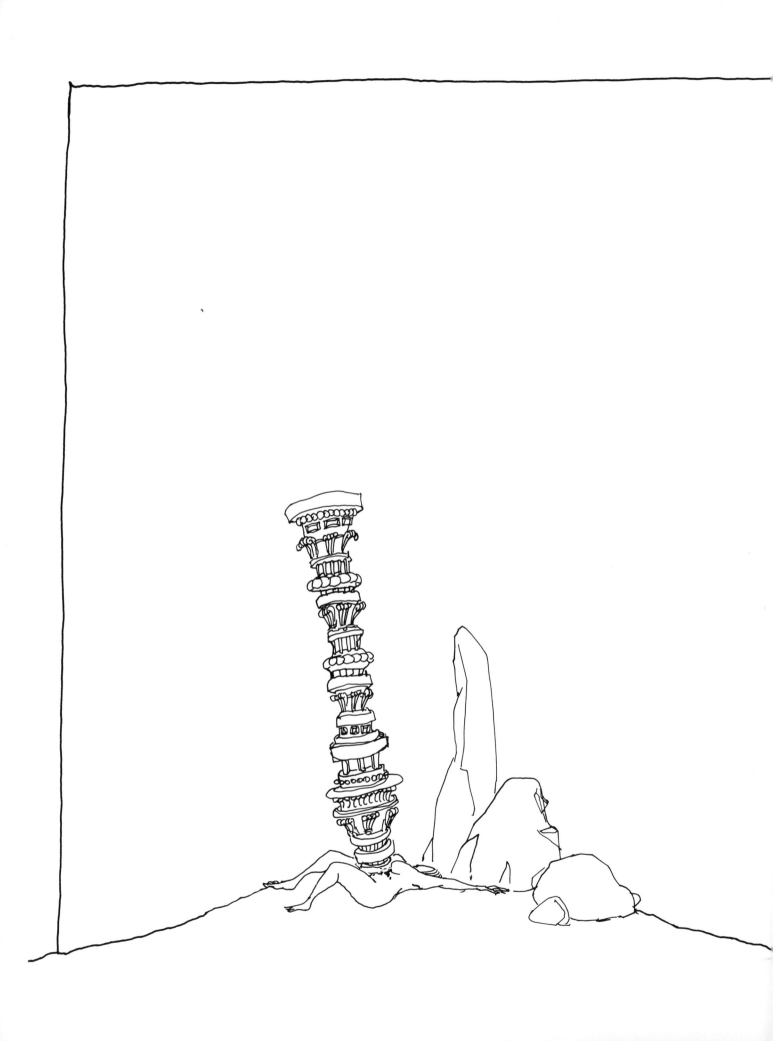

The Humorist and the Editor

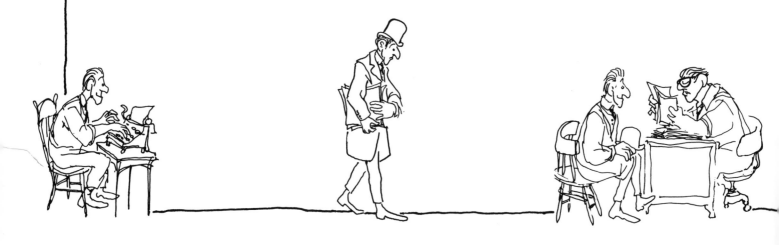

TO PLEASE A LADY

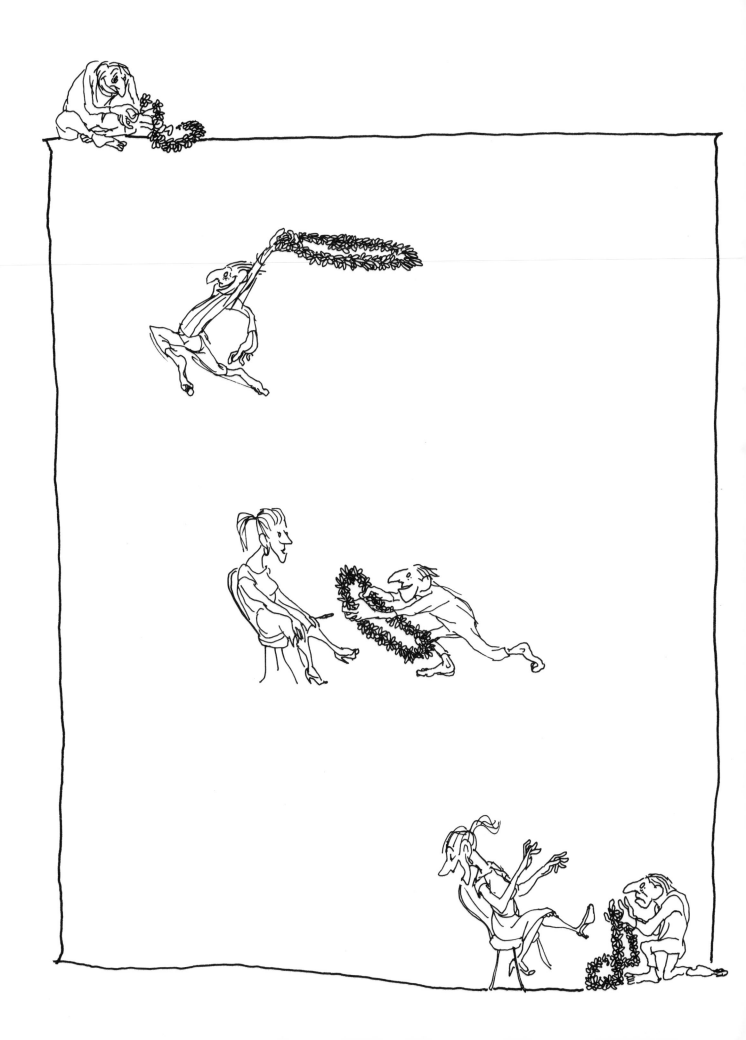

SHE ENTERS MY LIFE

ME
ME
WE

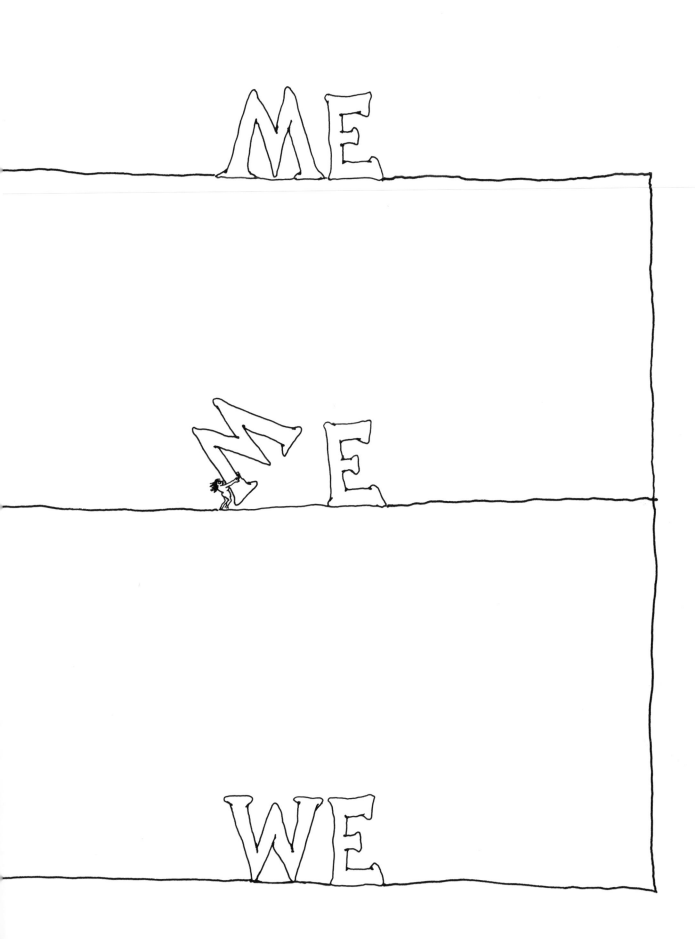

THE DEADLY WEAPON

TAKING TURNS

TEACH YOUR CHILDREN WELL

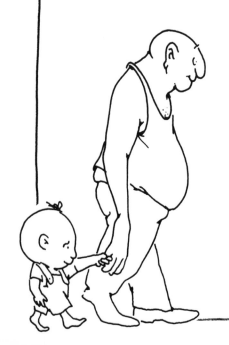

SONOFABITCH
PANSYWHORE
FREAKOJAPNIP
KRAUTREDPINKO
DIKEKIKEFROGHONKY
SPICCOONFAGGOTGINZO
REDNECKEGGHEADSHEENY
GREASERCHINKCOMMIEGOOK
KIKENIGGERPOLLACKDAGOS POPE LOVERS

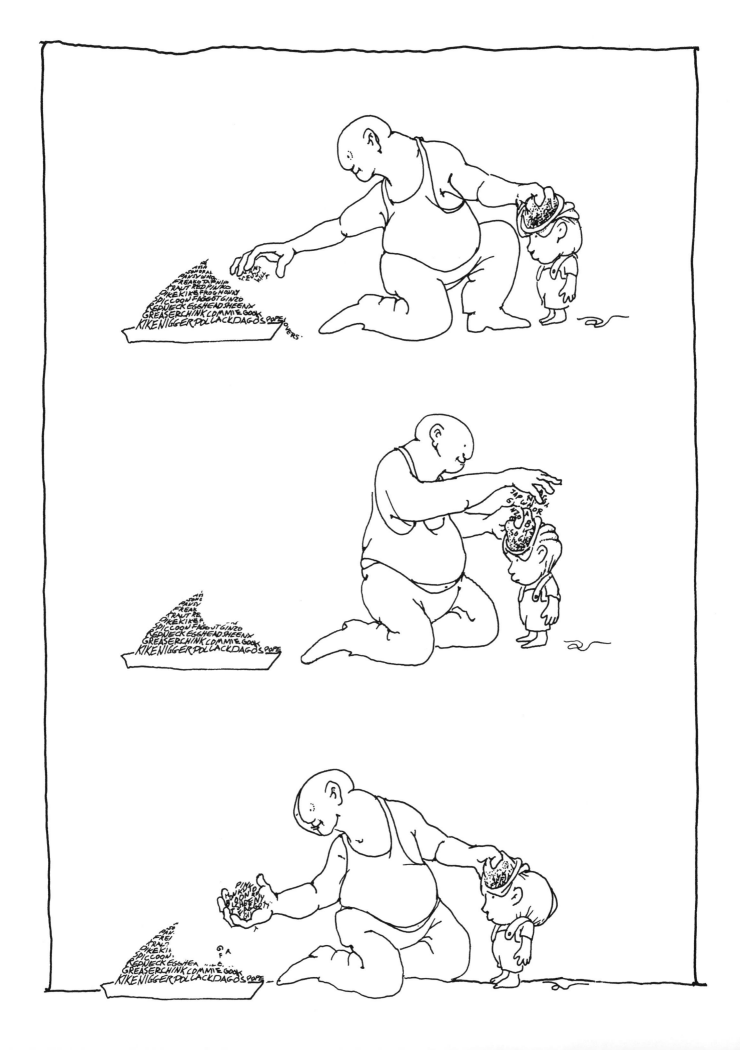

GREASERCH
KIKENIGGERPOLLACKDAGOSPOPE
KIKENIGGERPOL DAGOSPOPE
KIKENIGGERPOL DAGOSPOPE

THE ESCAPE

TERRITORIAL RIGHTS

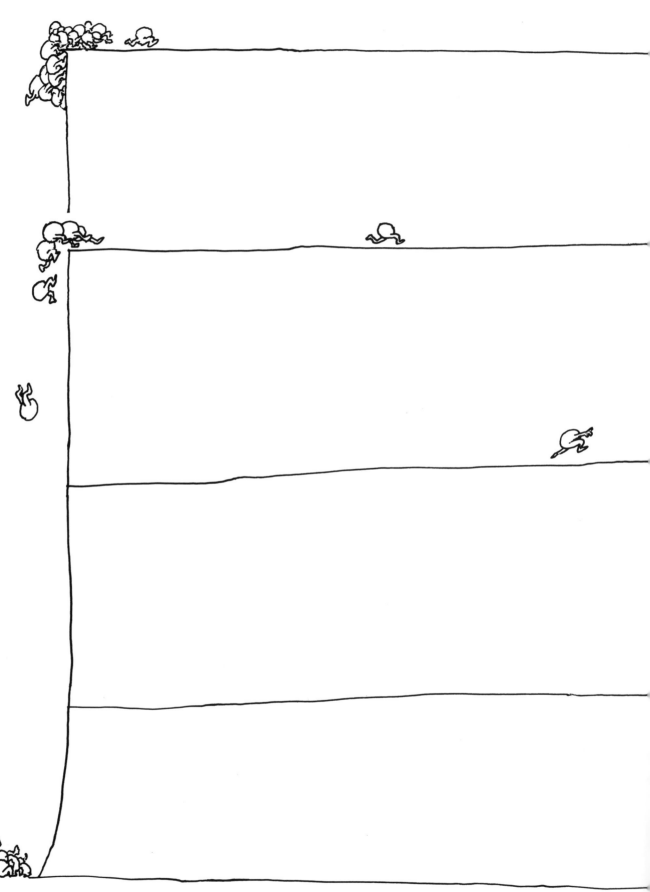

THE SPERM, THE EGG.

. . . AND THE PILL

THE MAN WHO INVENTED FIRE

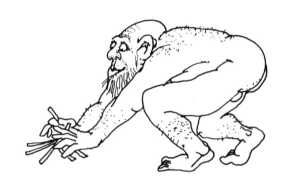

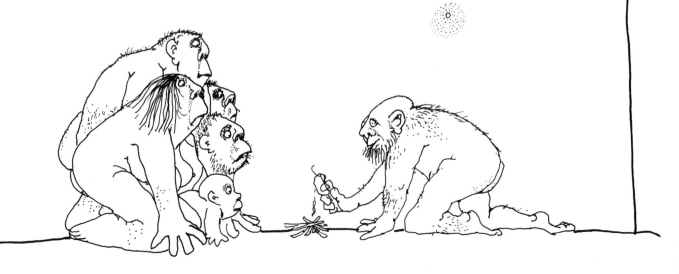

BABY'S FIRST WORDS

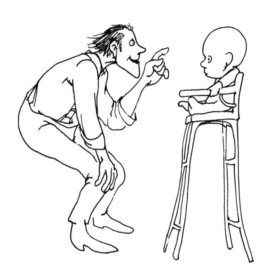

DA
DADADADA
DADA

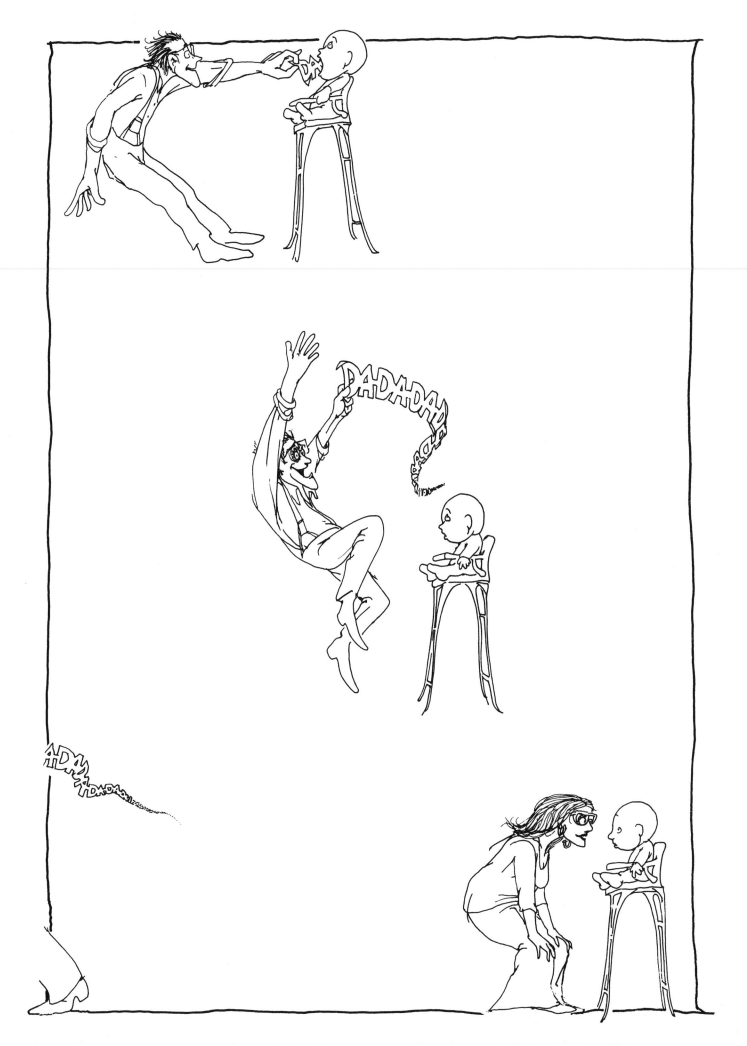

MA
MAMA

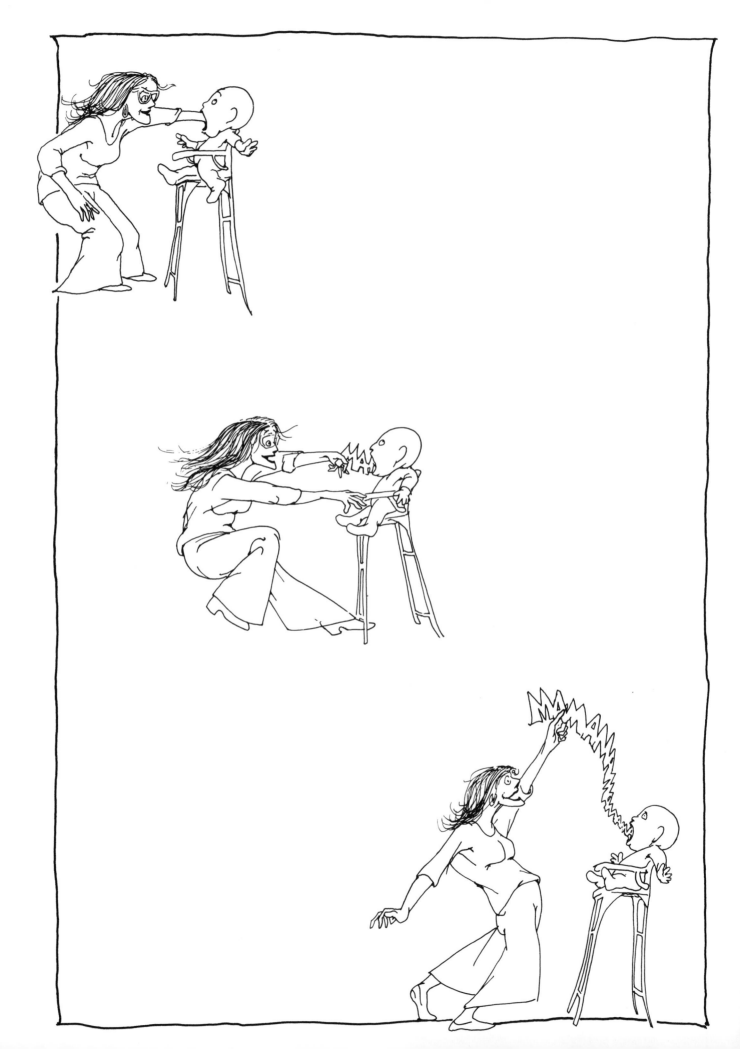

MAMAMAM
FUCK

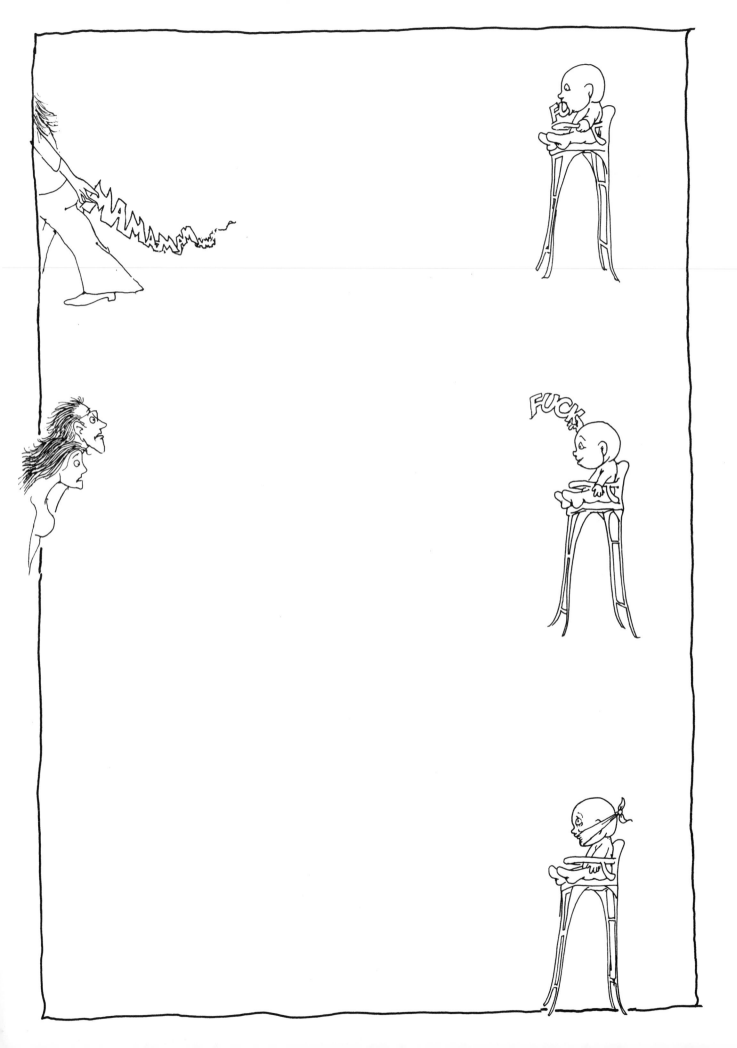

A COMFORTABLE RELATIONSHIP

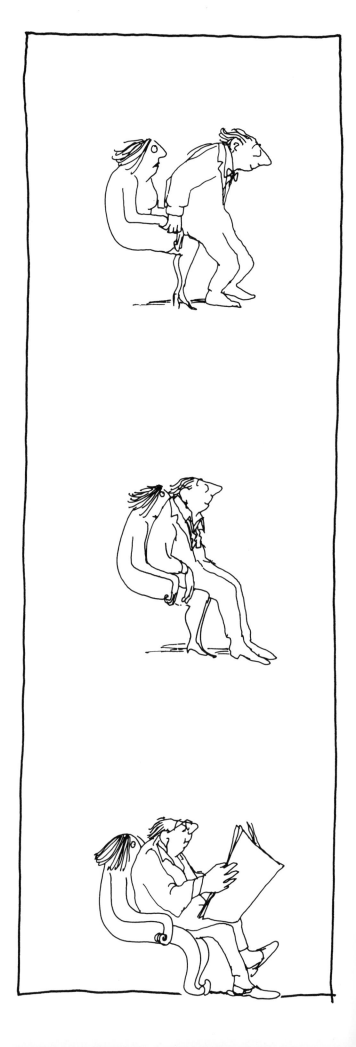

THE BANK ROBBER

PERSONNEL
PERSONNEL
IN
OUT

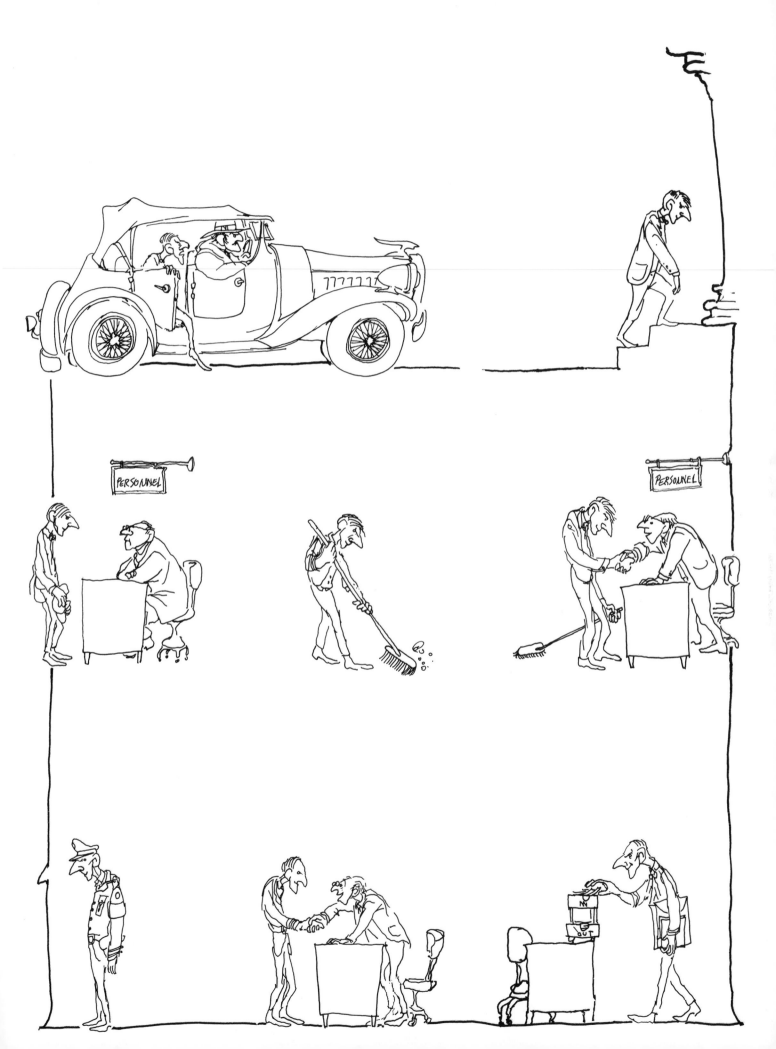

FILES
TELLER
ACCOUNTING
LOANS
VICE PRESIDENT
PRESIDENT

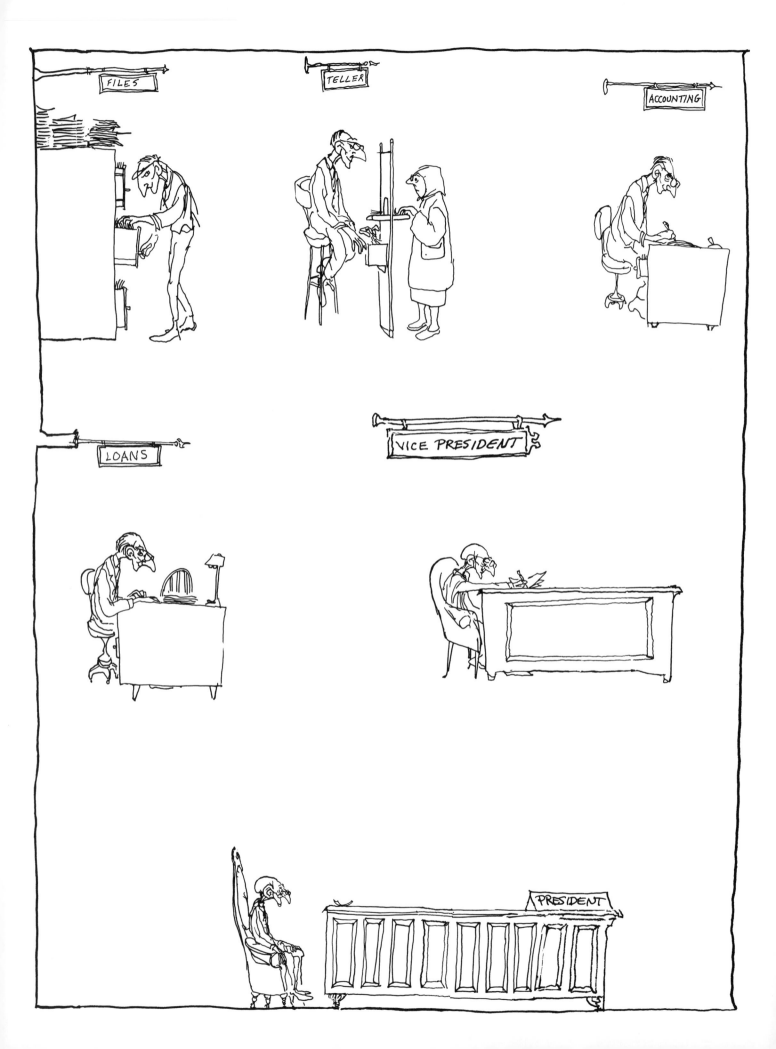

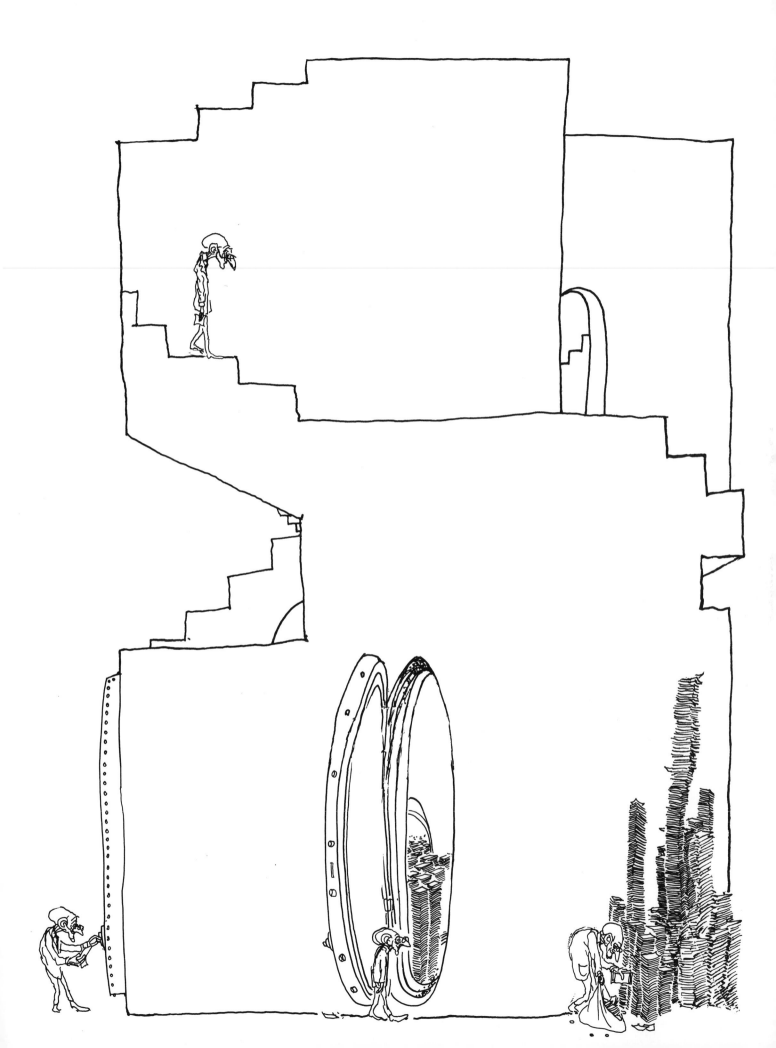

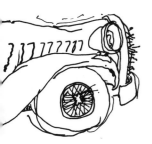

THE FLASHER

THE BRIDGE

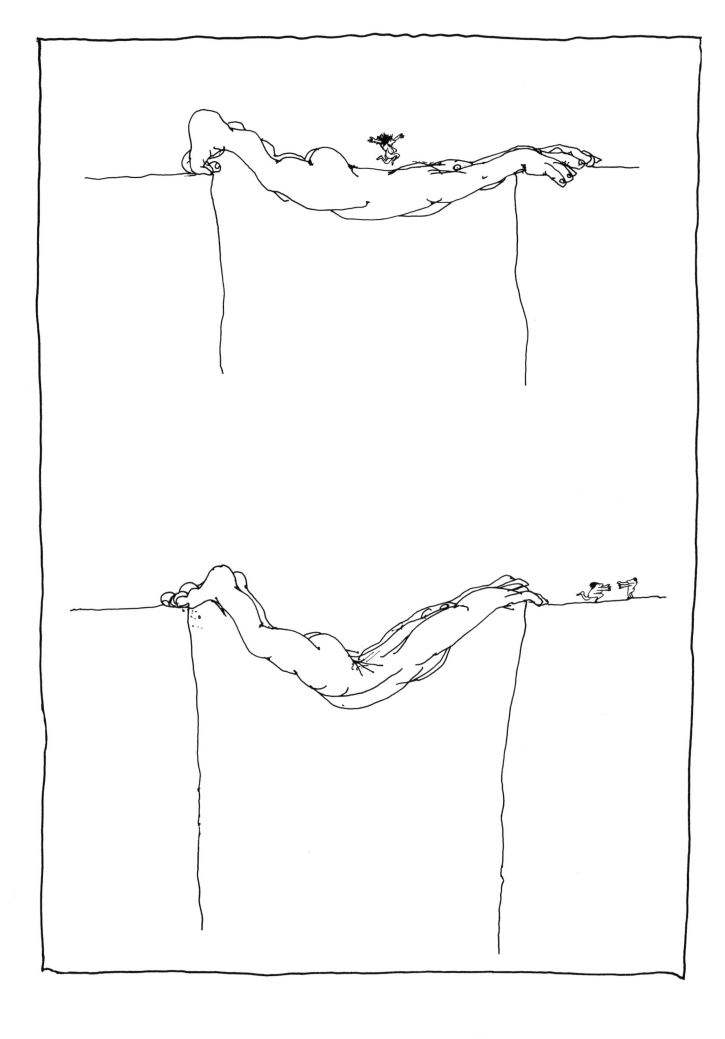

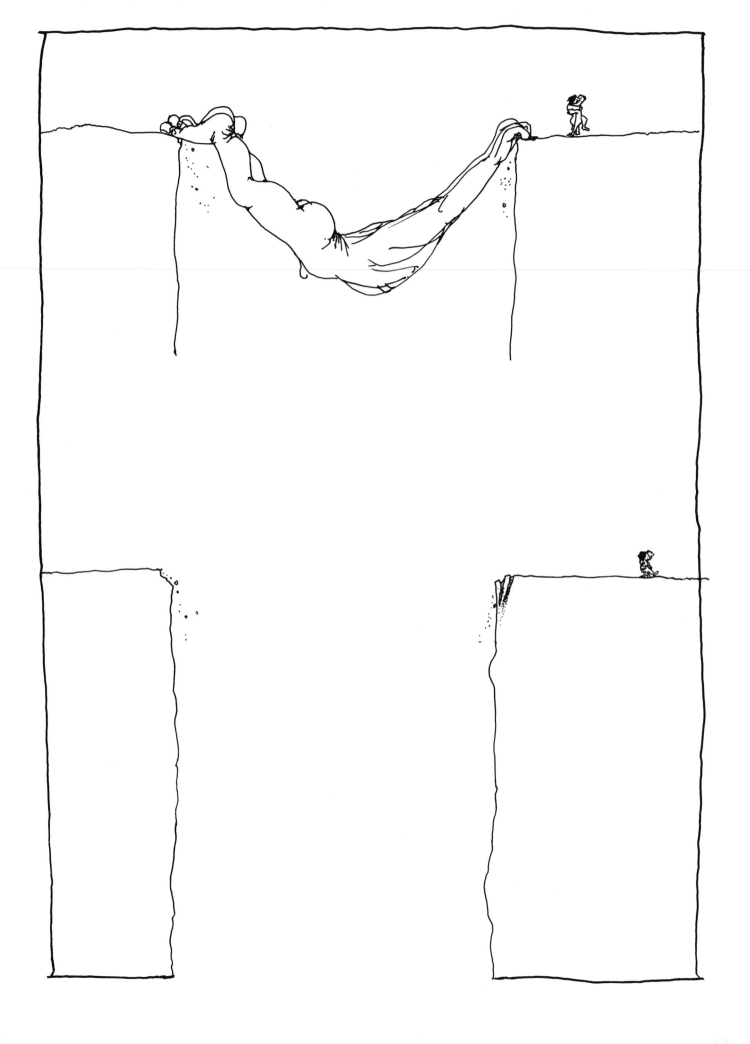

SUPPORTING THE FAMILY

H
W

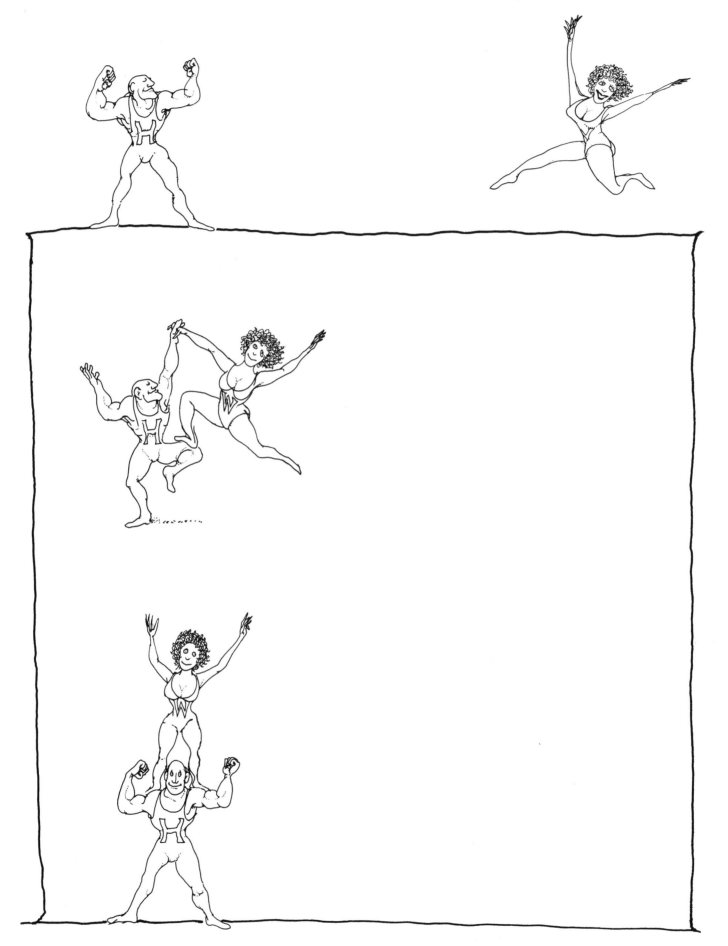

DOES A TREE . FALLING . . ALONE . . . IN A FOREST

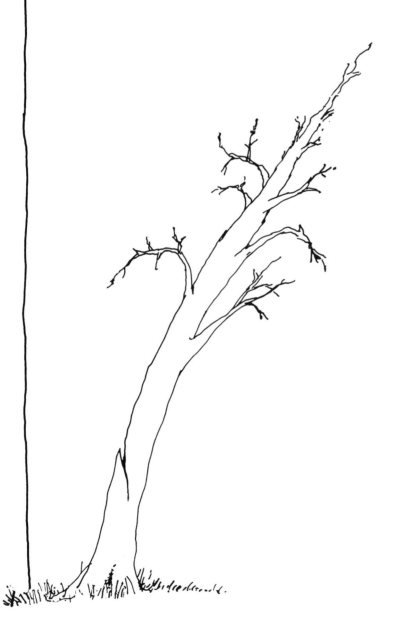

. . . MAKE ANY SOUND?
SHIT!

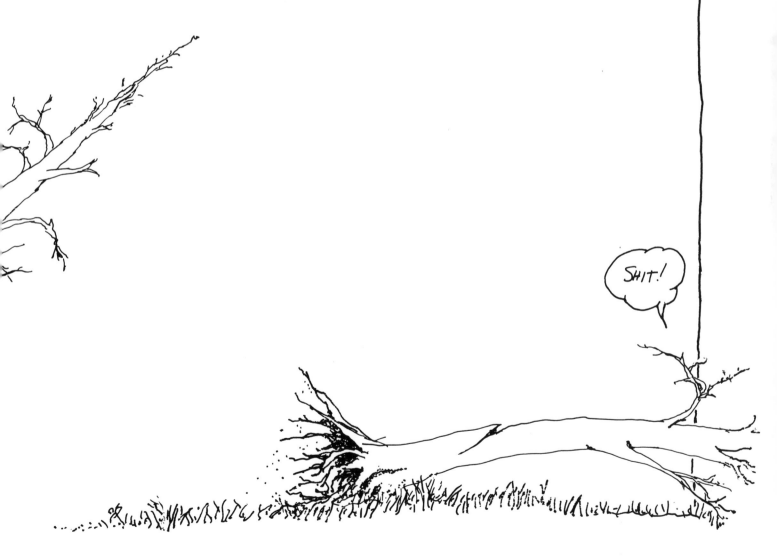

THE

SPLIT

THE FANTASY DIET

THE FOLLOWER

SOME ENCHANTED EVENING

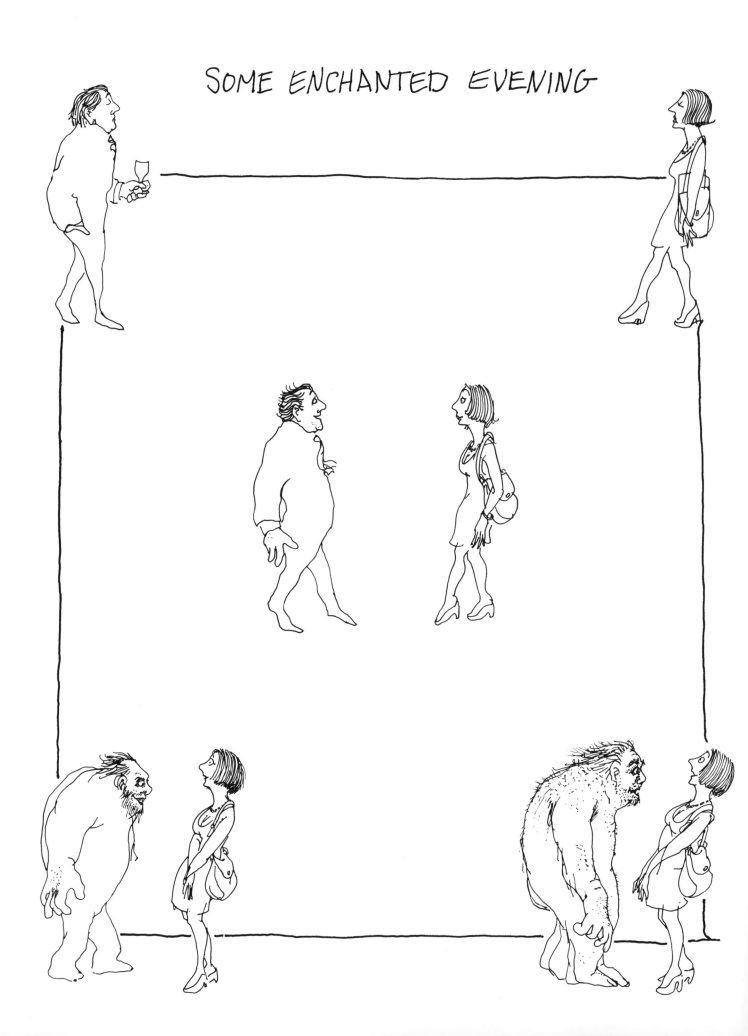

THE BRICK LAYER

THE QUEST OF THE HORSE'S ASS

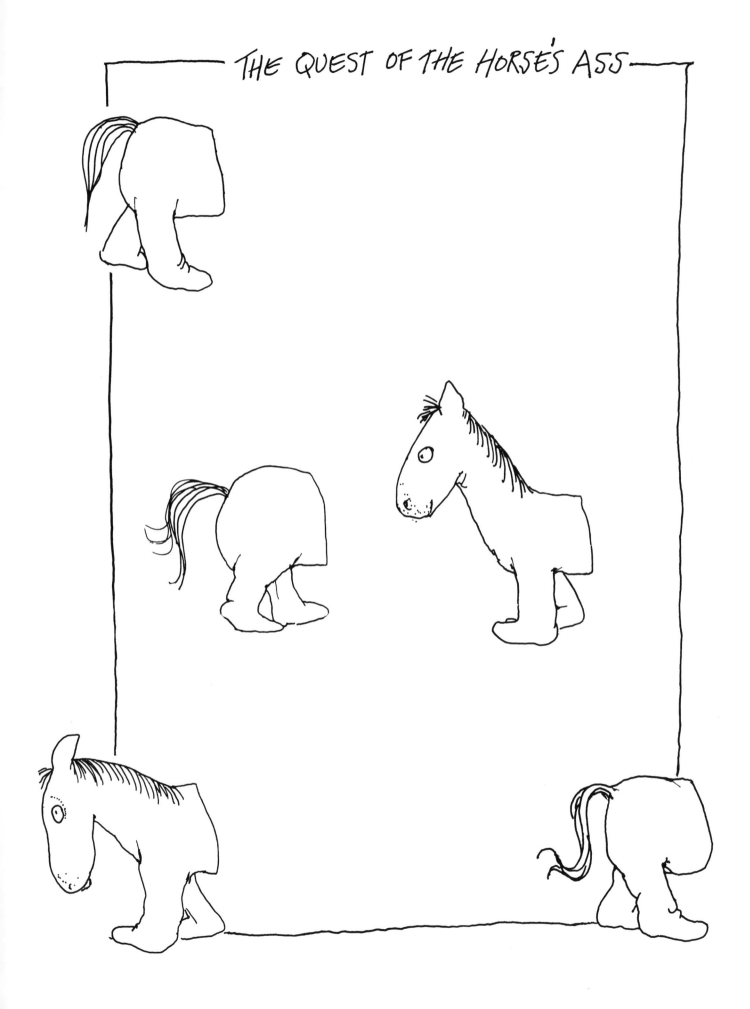

THE TWENTY COMMANDMENTS
THOU SHALT NOT KILL
THOU SHALT NOT COMMIT ADULTERY
THOU SHALT NOT STEAL
THOU SHALT NOT BEAR FALSE WITNESS AGAINST THY NEIGHBOR
THOU SHALT NOT COVET THY NEIGHBORS HOUSE
THOU SHALT NOT COMPROMISE
THOU SHALT NOT JUDGE
THOU SHALT NOT SEEK REWARDS
THOU SHALT NOT FOLLOW LEADERS
MIND THINE OWN BUSINESS

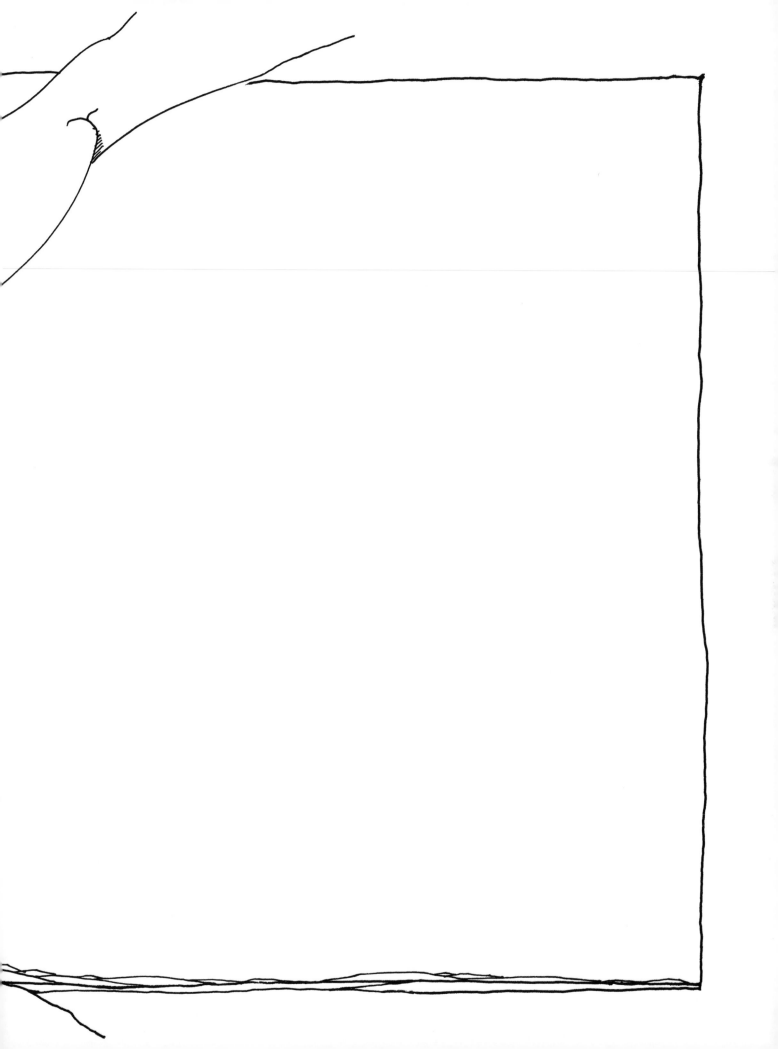

SHALT
NO OTHER GODS
BEFORE ME
THOU SHALT NOT MAKE UNTO THEE ANY GRAVEN IMAGE
THOU SHALT NOT TAKE THE NAME OF THE LORD THY GOD IN VAIN
REMEMBER THE SABBATH DAY TO KEEP IT HOLY
HONOR THY FATHER AND THY MOTHER
THOU SHALT NOT KILL
THOU SHALT NOT COMMIT ADULTERY
THOU SHALT NOT STEAL
THOU SHALT NOT BEAR FALSE WITNESS AGAINST THY NEIGHBOR
THOU SHALT NOT COVET THY NEIGHBORS HOUSE OR THY NEIGHBORS WIFE
THOU SHALT NOT COMPROMISE
THOU SHALT NOT JUDGE
THOU SHALT NOT SEEK REWARDS
THOU SHALT NOT FOLLOW LEADERS
REMEMBER EVERY DAY TO KEEP IT HOLY
HONOR THY CHILDREN
THOU SHALT NOT DESTROY THY BODY BEFORE ITS TIME
MIND THINE OWN BUSINESS
THOU SHALT NOT WASTE THY TIME
THOU SHALT NOT LAY GUILT UPON THE HEAD OF THY NEIGHBOR

THOU SHALT NOT COMPROMISE
THOU SHALT NOT JUDGE
THOU SHALT NOT SEEK REWARDS
THOU SHALT NOT FOLLOW LEADERS
REMEMBER EVERY DAY TO KEEP IT HOLY
HONOR THY CHILDREN
THOU SHALT NOT DESTROY THY BODY BEFORE IT'S TIME
MIND THINE OWN BUSINESS
THOU SHALT NOT WASTE THY TIME
THOU SHALT NOT LAY GUILT UPON THE HEAD OF THY NEIGHBOR
THOU SHALT HAVE NO OTHER GODS BEFORE ME
SHALT NOT MAKE UNTO ANY GRAVEN IMAGE
NOT TAKE THE LORD THY GOD
SABBATH
HOLY
FATHER
HY MOTHER
HALT NOT KILL
HALT NOT COMMIT
DULTERY
NOT STEAL
HALT NOT BEAR
WITNESS AGAINST
HY NEIGHBOR
HALT NOT COVET
HBORS HOUSE
Y NEIGHBORS

THE MAN WHO BELIEVED WHAT HE READ

WITH THE HELP OF A FRIEND, HE FINALLY CUTS THE CORD

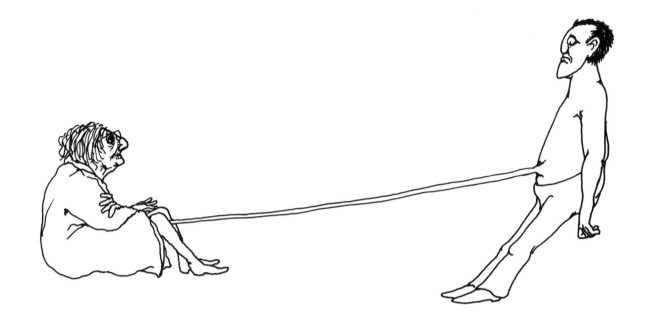

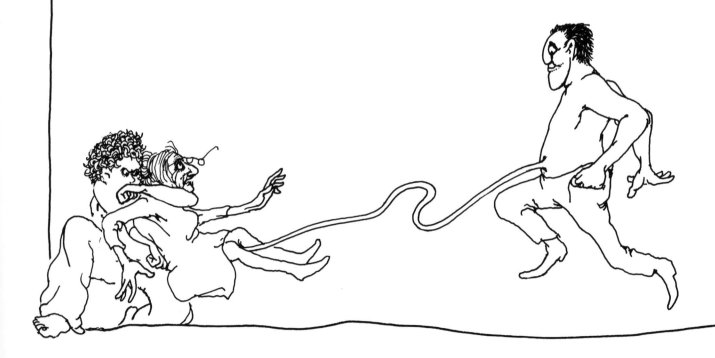

...AND HE HAS NEVER BEEN
HEARD FROM SINCE

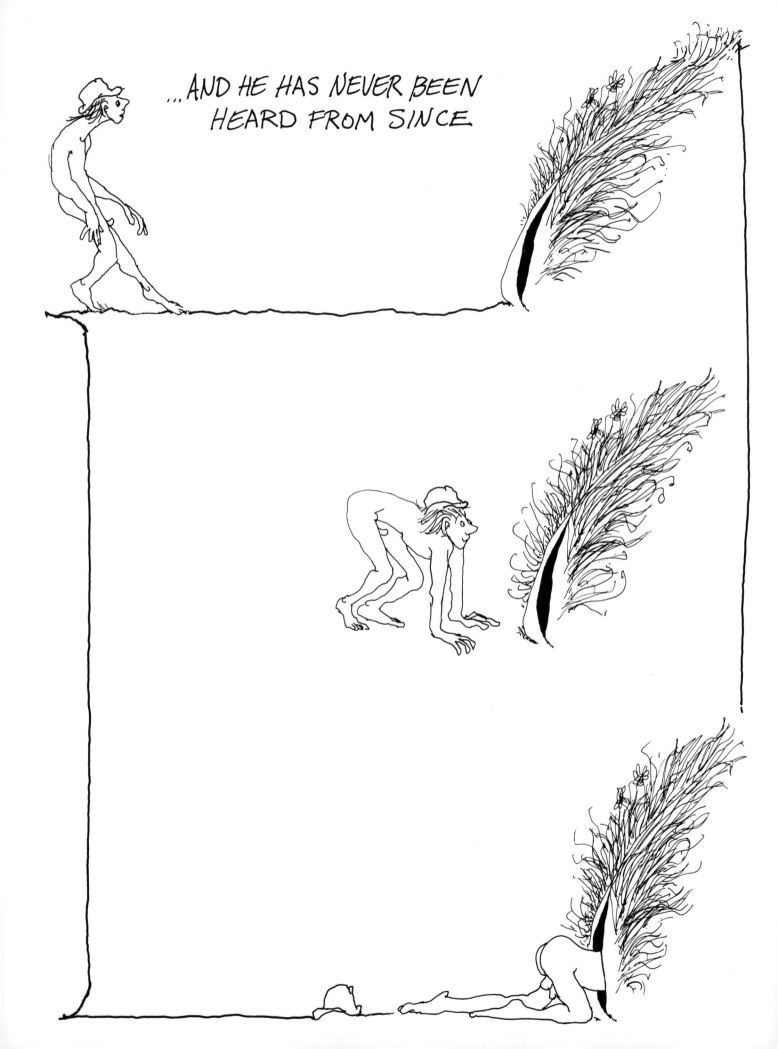

THE BLOW JOB

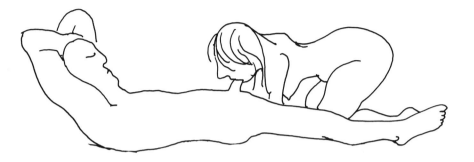

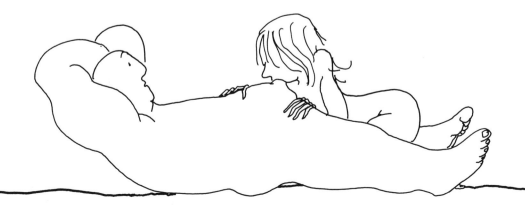

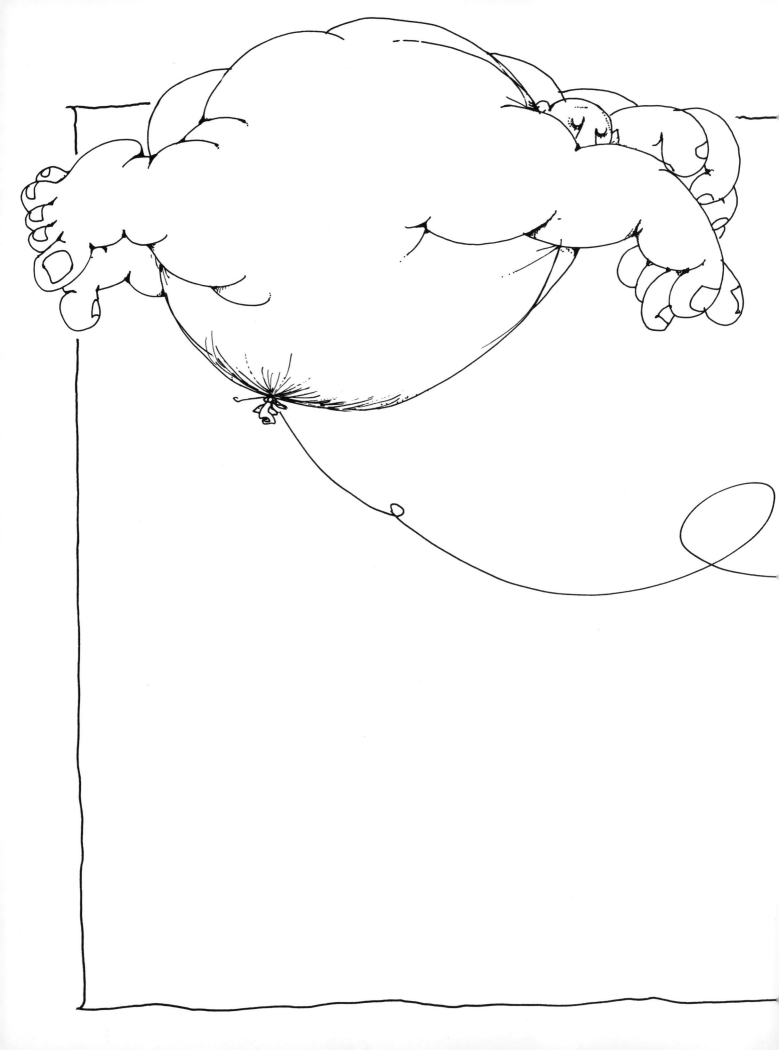

MY FEAR OF DENTISTS

I ACCEPT THE CHALLENGE

REAL MAN WANTED
REAL MAN WANTED
REAL MAN WANTED

REAL
MAN
WANTED

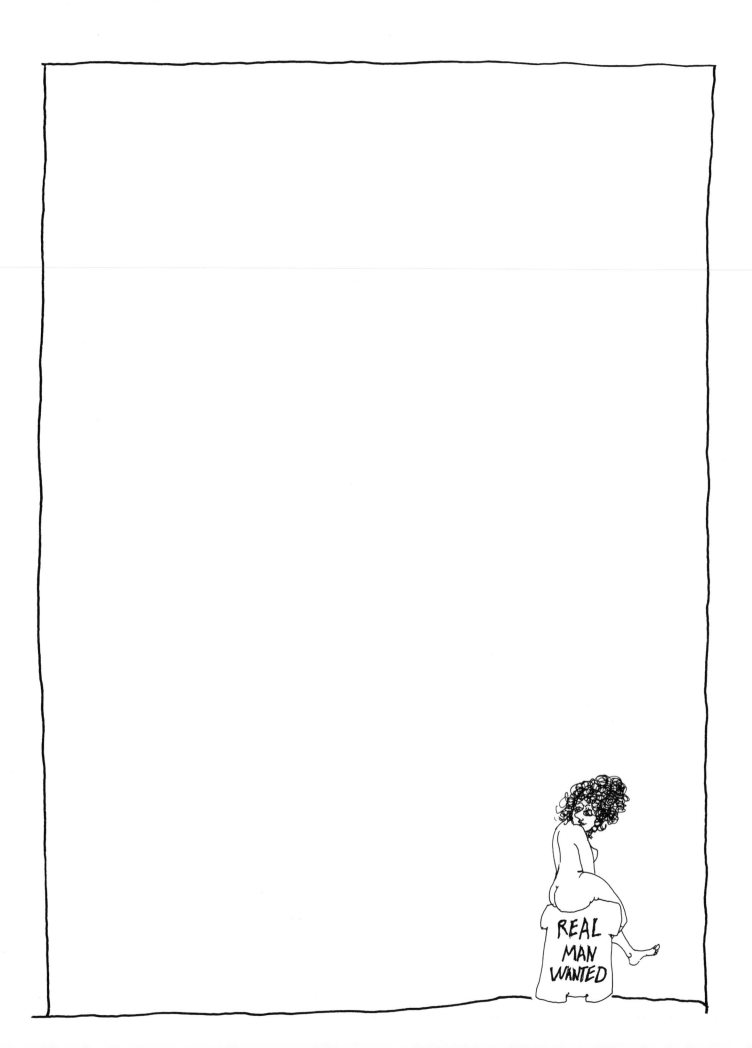

THE VOICE OF REASON

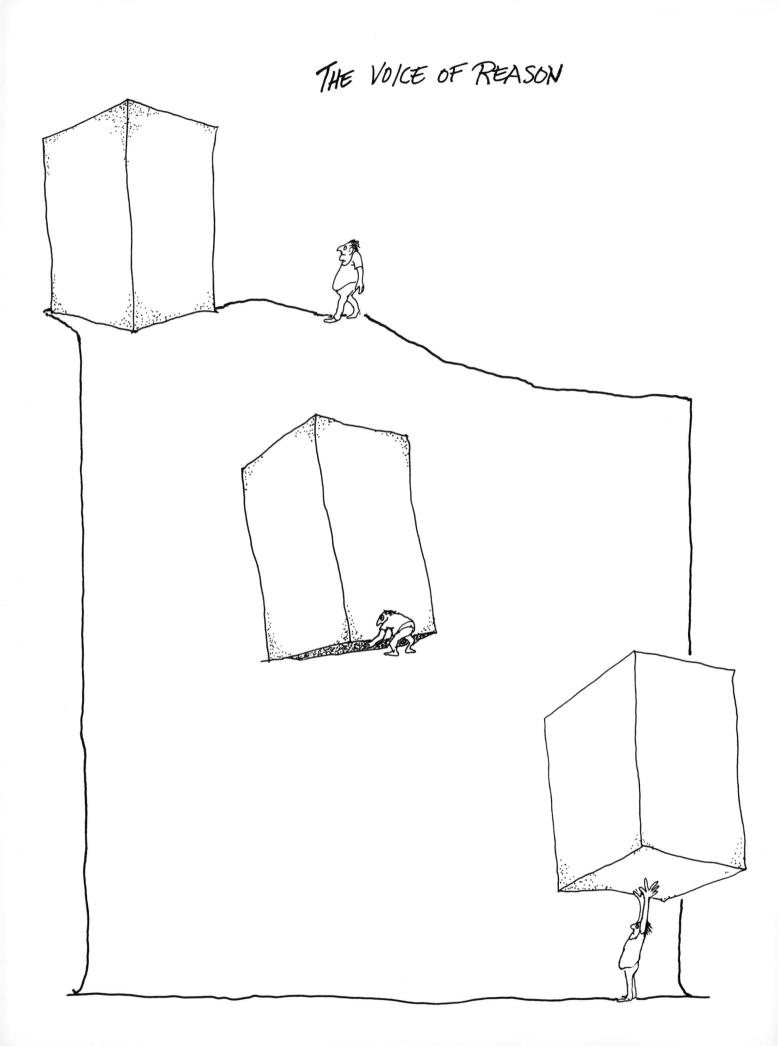

THE DOG LOVER

THE DISCIPLE

THE MAN...

THE STORM...

THE ANCHOR...

AND...THE FLOOD

THE LIFE AND DEATH
OF THE DILETTANTE

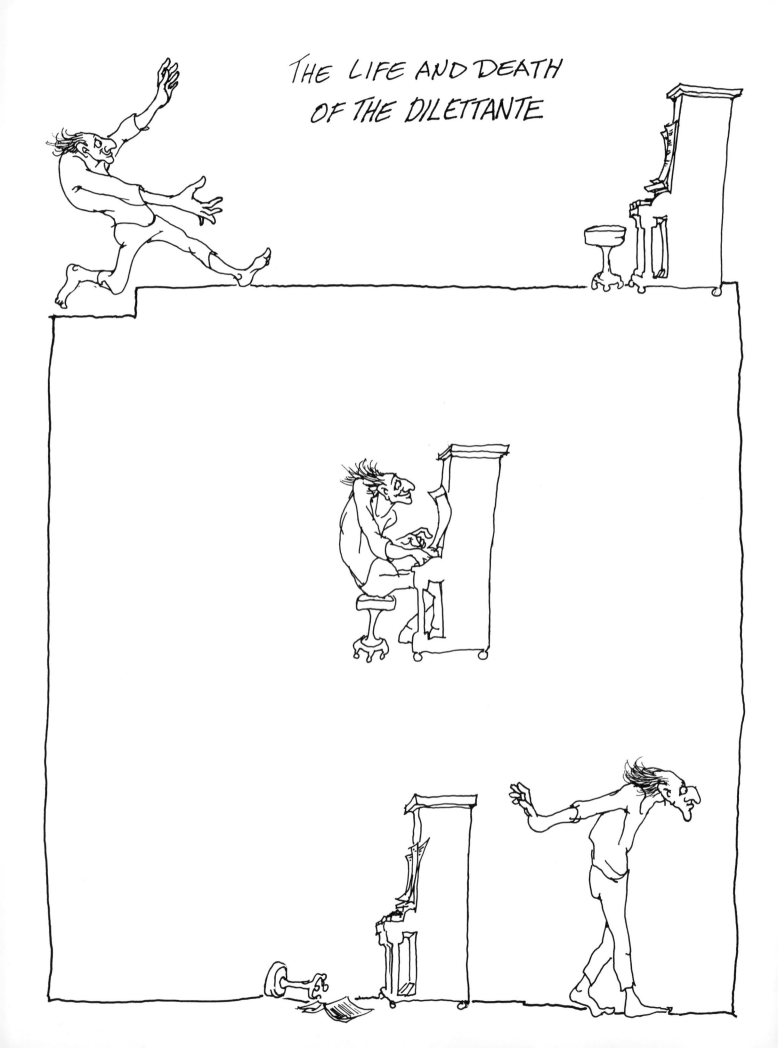

GIVING BIRTH . . .

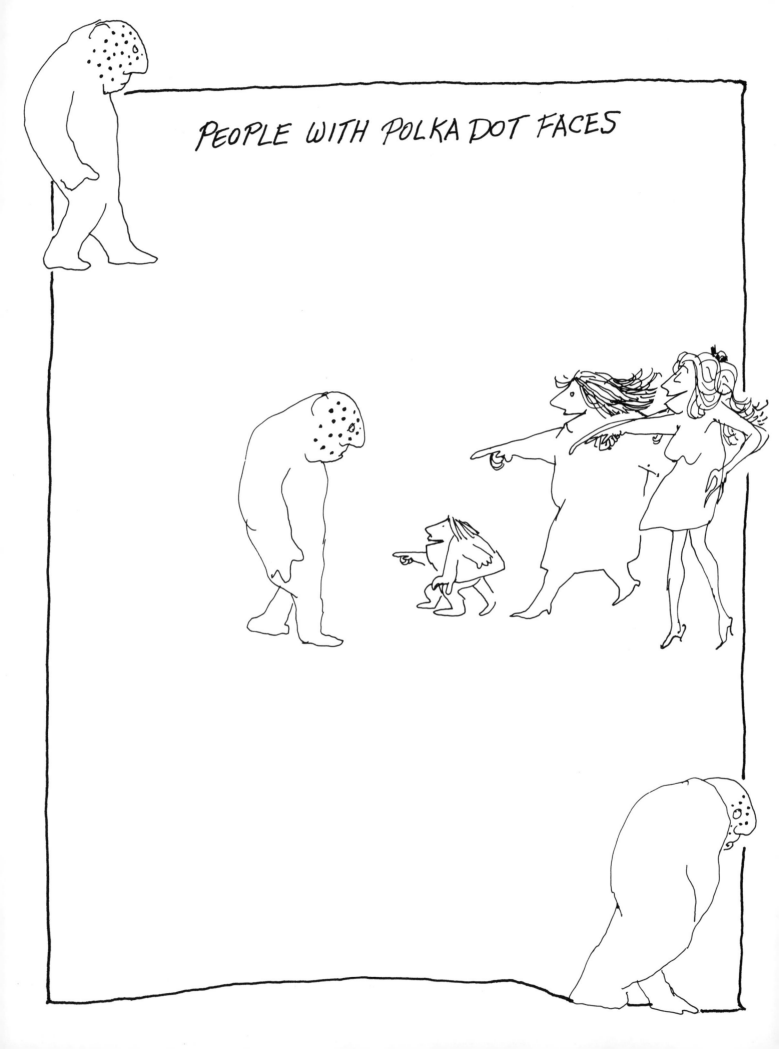

PEOPLE WITH POLKA DOT FACES

THE PENCIL WHO READ WHAT IT WROTE

therefore, it stands to reason that the only
effective method of effecting a genuine and
lasting political change is a deliberate

therefore, it stands to reason that the only
effective method of effecting a genuine and
lasting political change is a deliberate
and orderly effort by reasonable and
responsible individuals, working within
the system for the ~~whit~~ wait a minute—

therefore, it stands to reason that the only
effective method of effecting a genuine and
lasting political change is a deliberate
and orderly effort by reasonable and
responsible individuals, working wi
the system for the~~the~~ Wait a minute—
This is a crock of Shit— working
within the system be s a collaboration
with that system rage is impossible
what is needed total and dedicated
militant thrust

therefore, it stands to reason that the only
effective method of effecting a genuine and
lasting political change is a deliberate
and orderly effort by reasonable and
responsible individuals, working within
the system for the~~the~~ Wait a minute—
This is a crock of Shit— Any working
within the system becomes a collaboration
with that system and change is impossible
what is needed is a total and dedicated
militant thrust that would strike at
the very foundation of

therefore, it stands to reason that the only
effective method of effecting a genuine and
lasting political change, deliberate
and orderly effort by nable and
responsible individu orking within
the system for th sit a minute—
This is a crock hit — Any working
within the s em becomes a collaboration
with that.

therefore, it stands to reason that the
effective method of effecting a genu rd
lasting political change is a d te
and orderly effort by ress and
responsible individuals, within
the system for the y within

therefore, it stands to reason that the only
effective method of effecting a genuine and
lasting political change is a deliberate
and orderly effort by reasonable and
responsible individuals, working within
the system for the betterment of all mankind.

Of course a great deal of patience and wisdom
is necessary in this effort as well as a genuine
respect for the principles and traditions of the

SHE FINALLY

ST

PAS

GOT IT TOGETHER.

FU1

EUTURE

CRY FOR THE DEAD FLOWER

SHE   BEGAN   TO

GROW

AND

HE

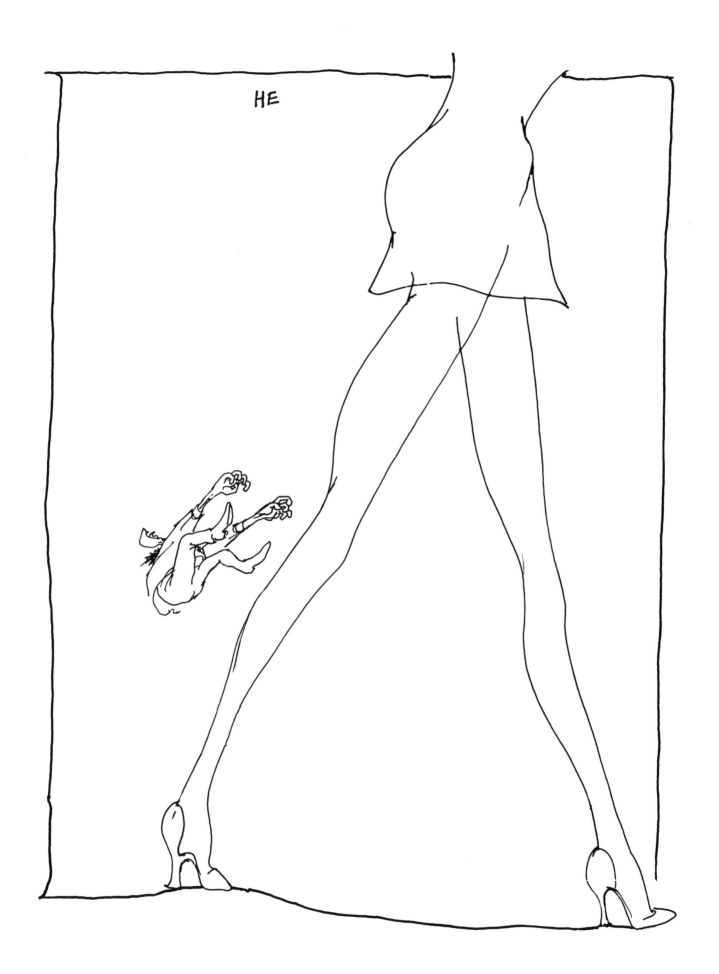

DIDN'T.

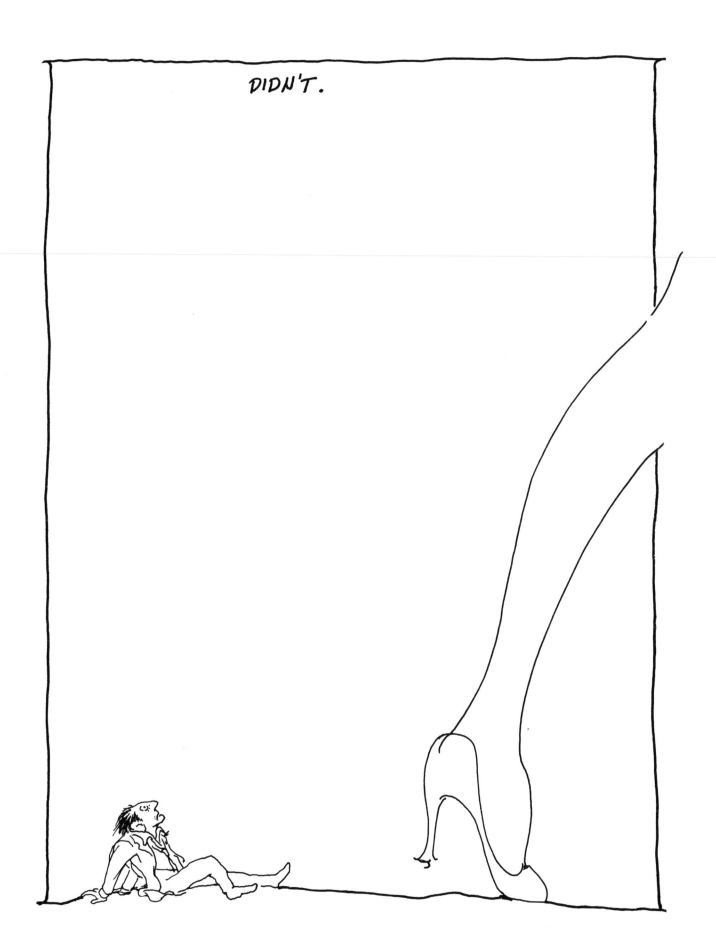

THE ACADEMIC PROCESS

GETTING HER AWAY FROM HER FAMILY

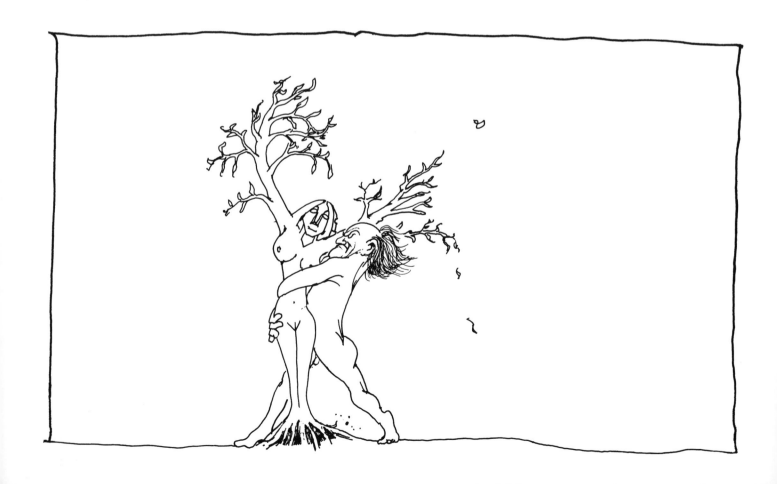

THE SELF SUFFICIENT

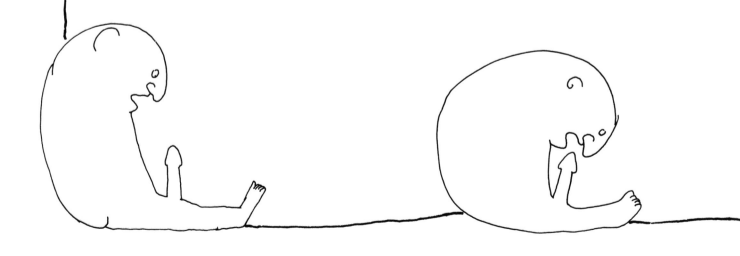

THEY FORGOT THE NAILS

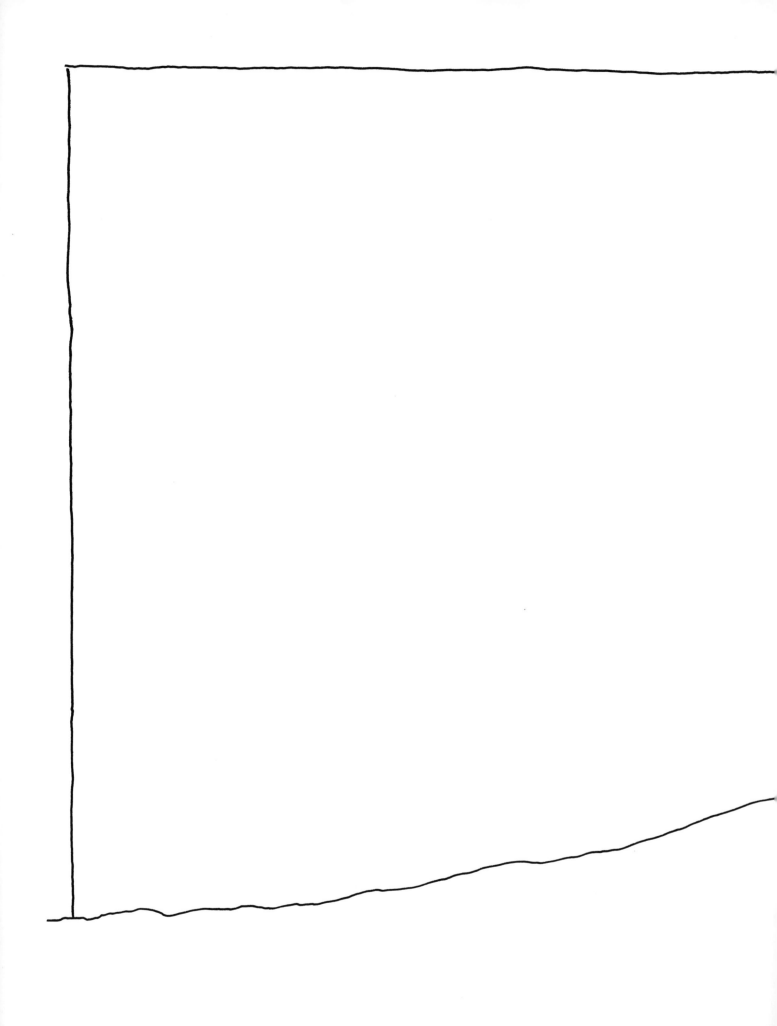

WOULD YOU STILL LOVE ME..?
YES-
YES -

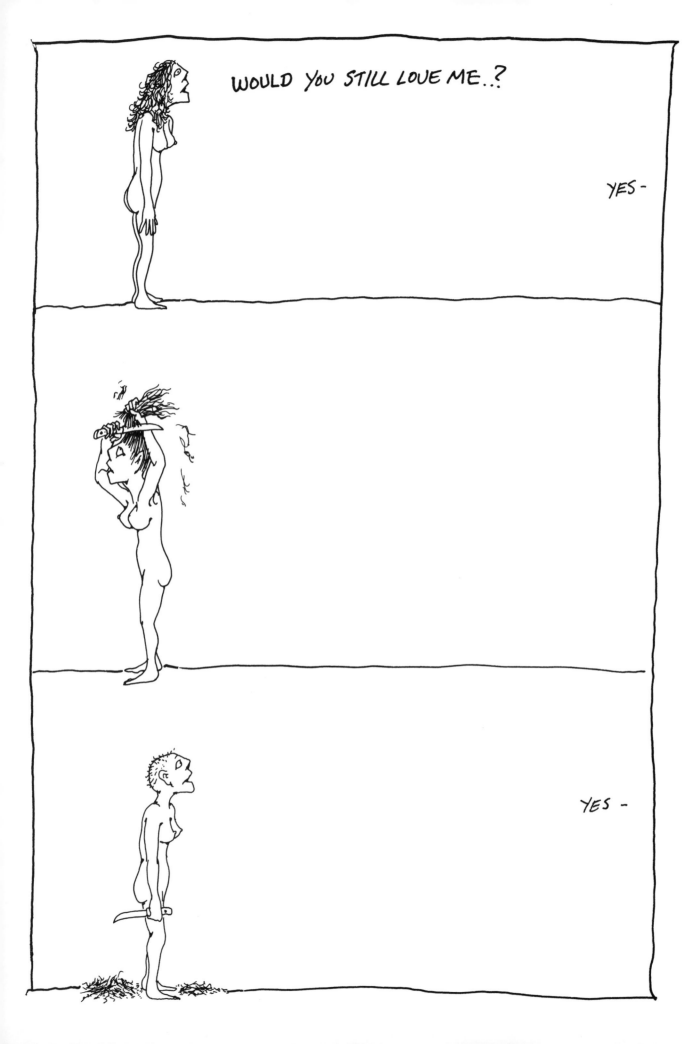

YES -

YES -

YES -

NO-
I KNEW IT!

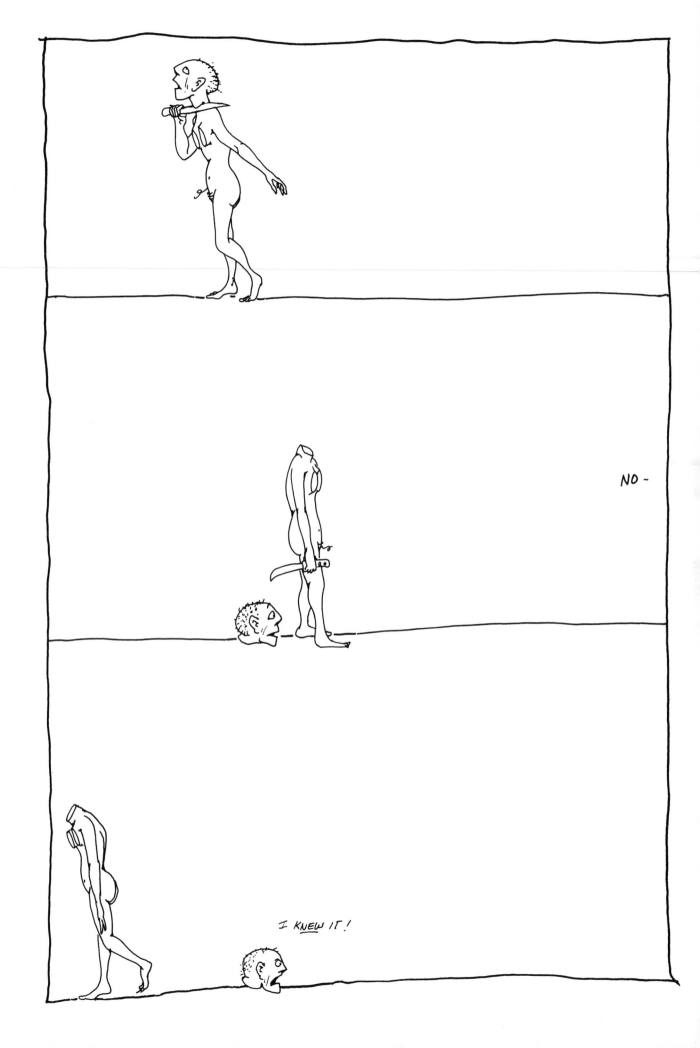

HOW THE BULLSHIT GROWS

ETC....

THE NERVOUS BREAKDOWN

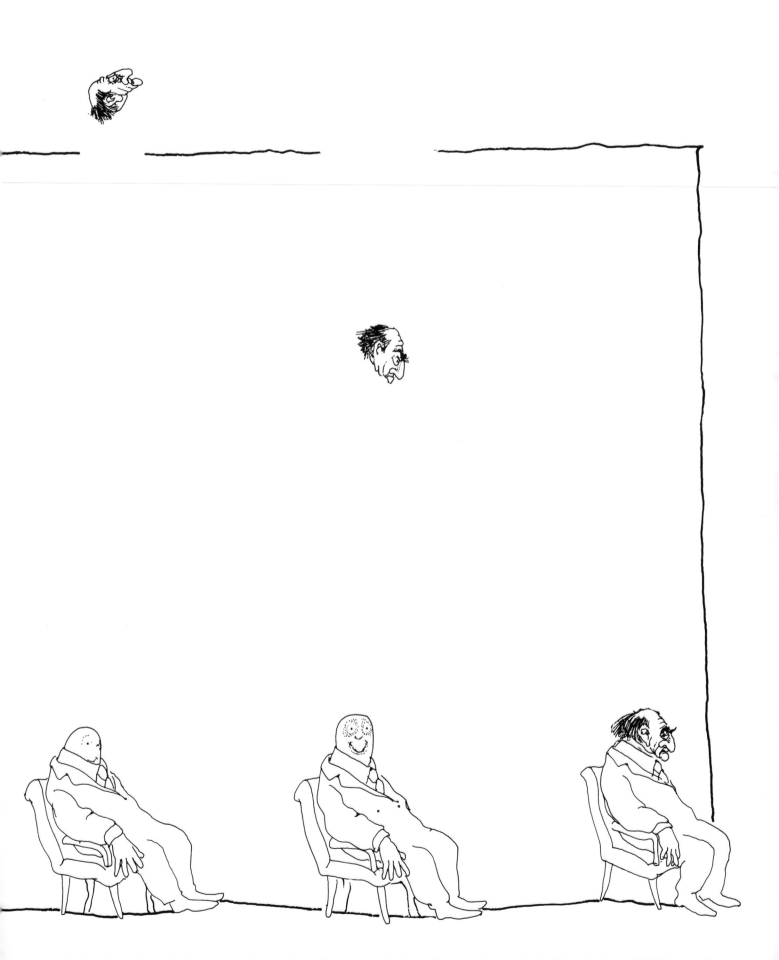

P. R.

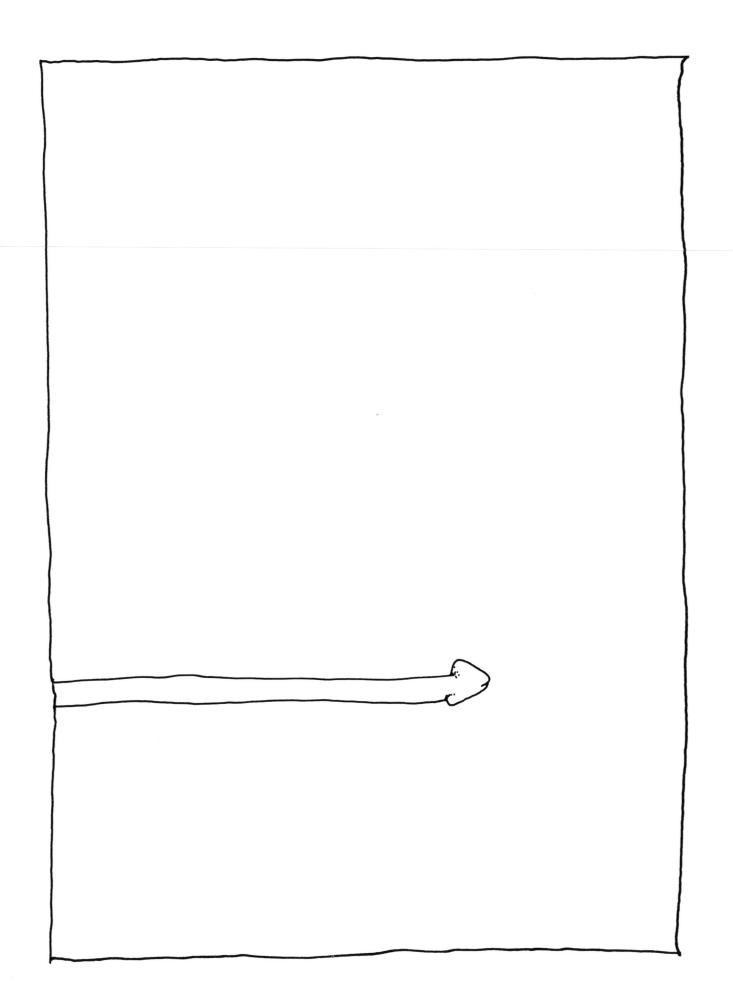

FREE ENTERPRISE

MOON INSIDE
SEE THE MOON
25¢

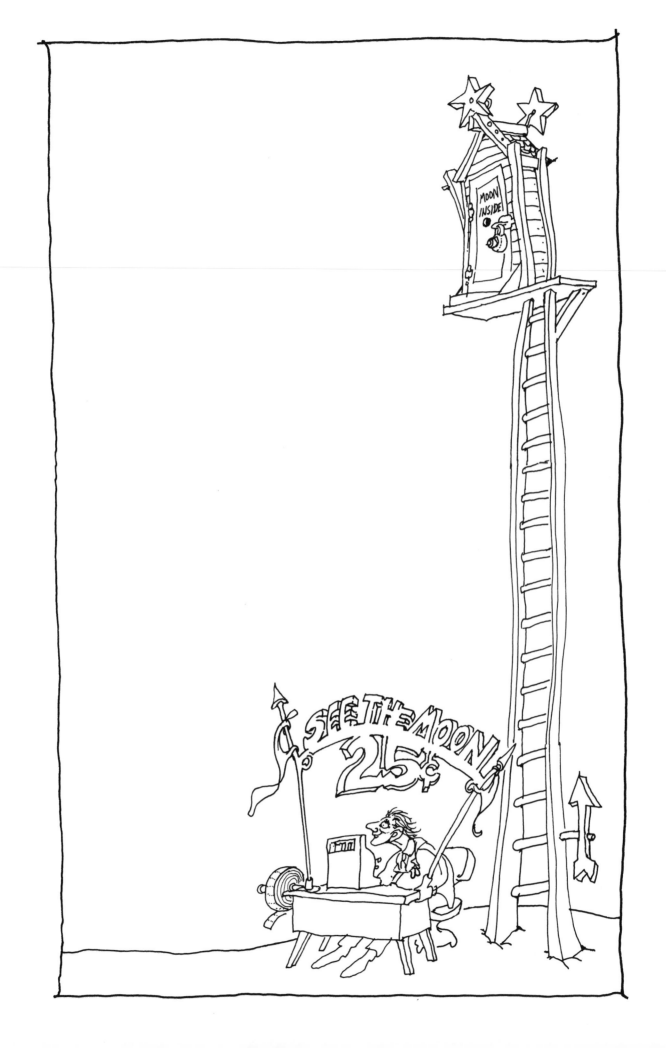

THE SUICIDE BULLET

THE SEARCH
FOR THE SCROLLS

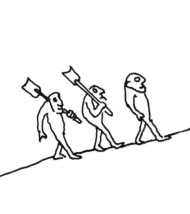

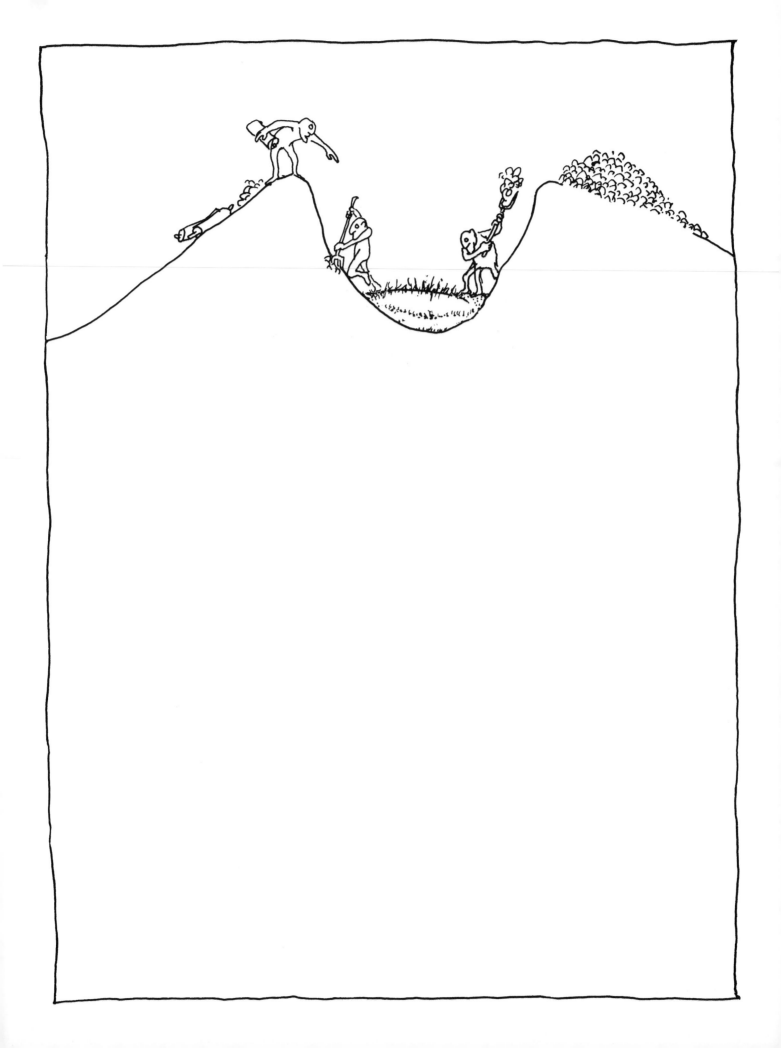

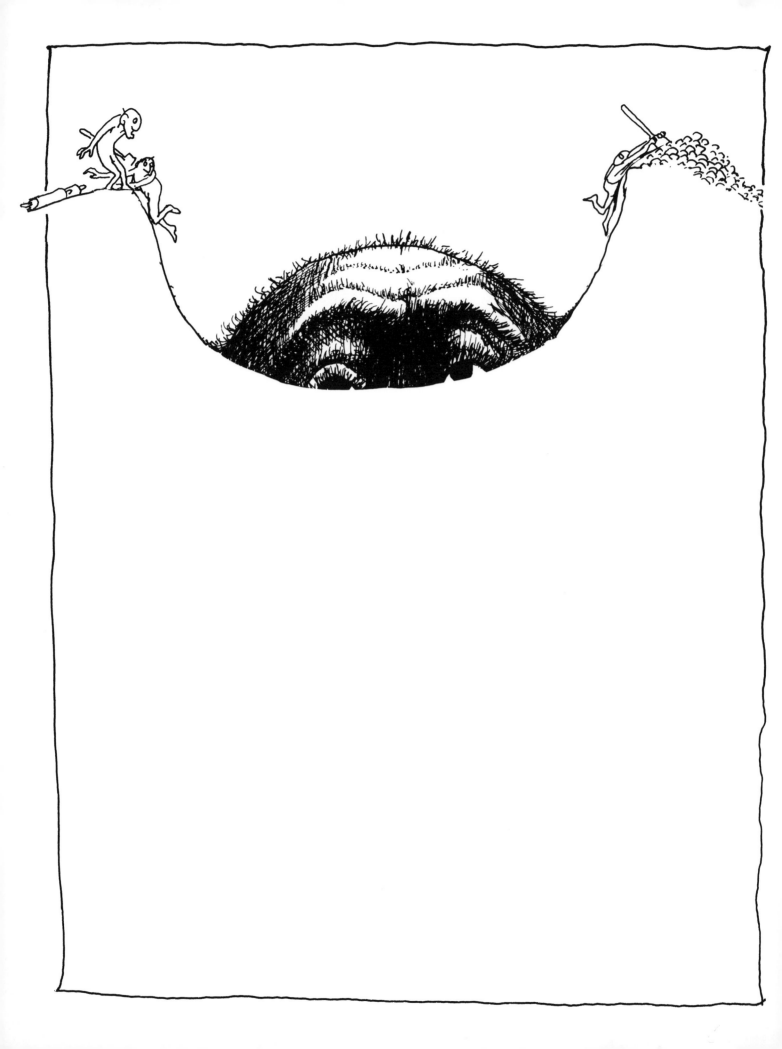

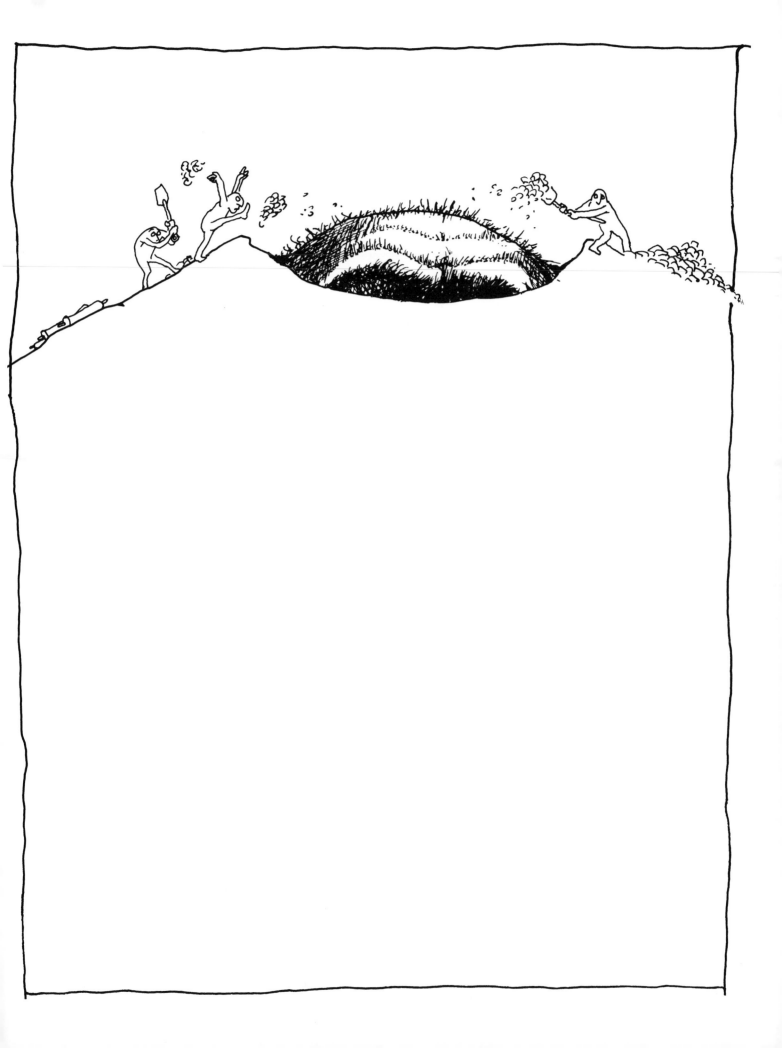

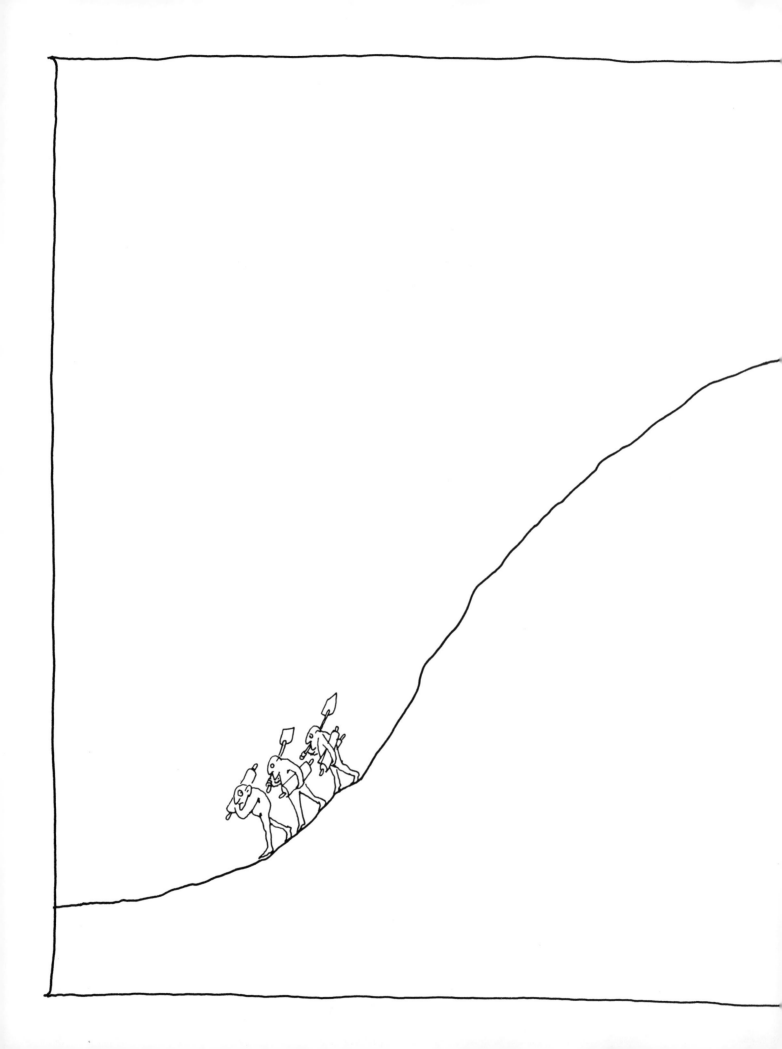

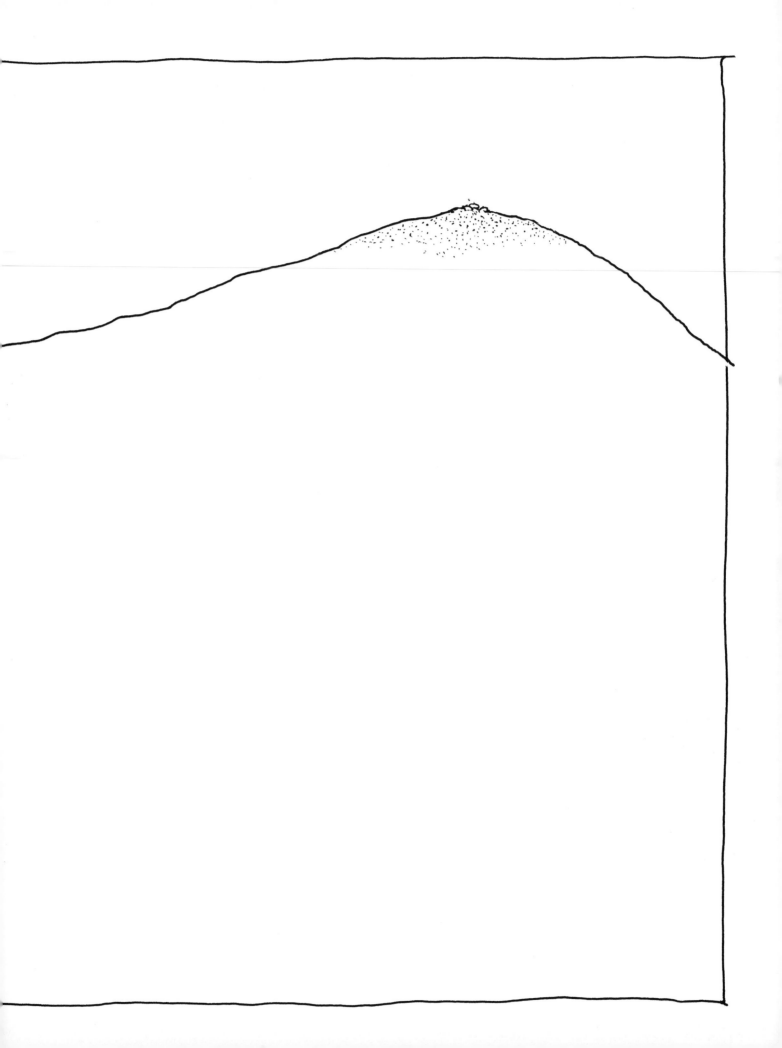

THE OLD MAN AND THE SWING

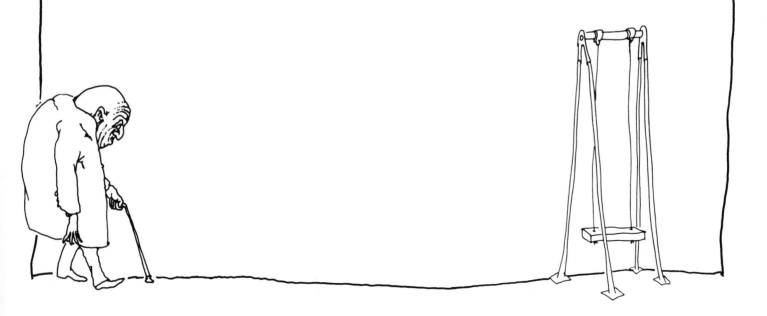

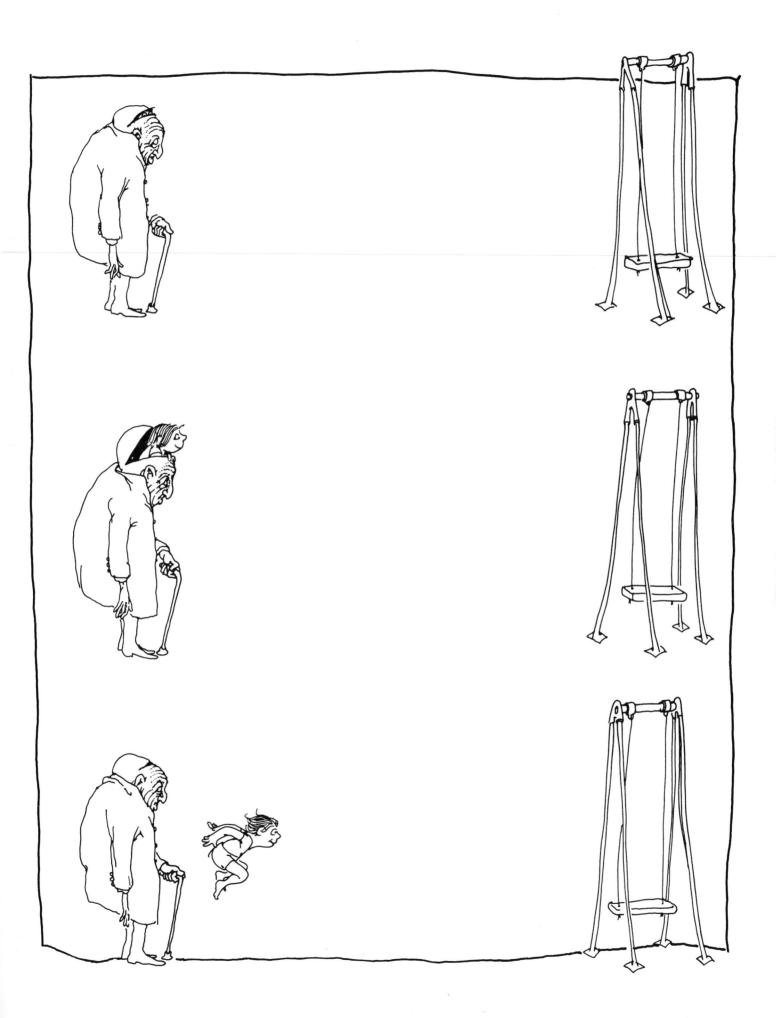

THE HAPPY ENDING

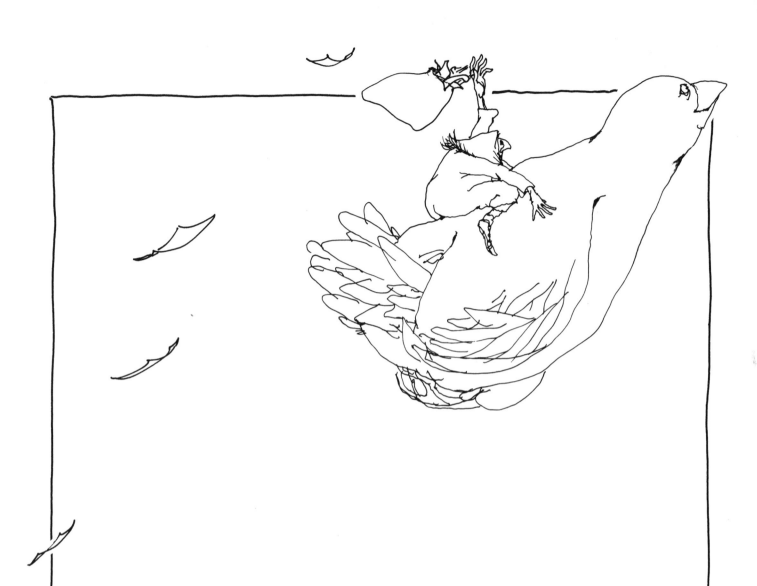

My thanks to —

Jonathan Dolger for the start,
Win Knowlton for the chance,
and Edite Kroll for the hard work and encouragement,

Shel Silverstein

Book lovingly designed by Ruth Bornschlegel